GEORGIA
FREE PERSONS
OF COLOR

Volume II

Appling, Camden, Clarke, Emanuel,

Jones, Pulaski, and Wilkes Counties

1818-1865

By
Michael A. Ports

CLEARFIELD

Reprinted for Clearfield Company by
Genealogical Publishing Company
Baltimore, Maryland
2015

ISBN 978-0-8063-5764-5

Introduction

In 1818, the Georgia legislature enacted a law requiring free persons of color to register with the inferior court of the county of their residence. Registers survive for only twenty-one of Georgia's counties. While the law required the inferior court clerks to maintain registers with the names, ages, places of nativity, residence, time of coming into the state, and occupation of each free person of color, an evaluation of the surviving registers reveals very little consistency in either format or information recorded between the various counties or even within a particular county over time. The following transcriptions of the registers from seven counties, Appling, Camden, Clarke, Emanuel, Jones, Pulaski and Wilkes, were made from the microfilm copies of the original records available in the microfilm reading room of the Georgia Department of Archives and History, Morrow, Georgia. The same microfilm is available from the Family History Library in Salt Lake City. The transcription of the register from Morgan County was made from the original record volume held by the Georgia archives.

Overall, the quality of the microfilm is good and the handwriting of the various court clerks is legible, making the transcription straightforward and not too difficult. However, ink blots, smears, clerks scribbling, as well as imperfect film exposure, occasionally make transcribing the records problematic, such problems noted between brackets, for example [smudge] or [illegible]. The transcriptions follow Sperry's recommended guidelines for reading early American script.[1] Researchers should consult the microfilm, or even the original records, to either confirm the transcription or formulate alternative interpretations of the handwriting.

Because the seven county registers differ in both format and information recorded, subsequent county chapters each include an introduction explaining the format and content of each transcription. Throughout the original registers, the various clerks made extensive use of both ditto marks and the letters "Do" or "do" to indicate a duplication of a previous entry, the subsequent transcription repeating the previous entry in full. For consistency and to avoid confusion, the transcriptions spell out the names of states, counties, and cities, regardless of how the names are abbreviated. Also, Georgia is not repeated after the names of counties located within the state. In a similar manner, the transcriptions simplify the suffixes Jr. and Sr., regardless of how they appear in the original record. Dates are presented in a consistent format, regardless of how they appear in the original. Occupations also are standardized. For example, blacksmith is preferred over black smith, blk smith, etc. All names are transcribed as accurately as possible, misspellings not corrected no matter how obvious the error. Researchers should consult the original record or microfilm copy to either confirm the transcription or formulate alternative interpretations of the information in the registers.

A brief synopsis of the Georgia laws governing manumissions and the registration of free persons of color follows the Introduction. Also included is a partial list of the manumissions issued by the Georgia state legislature from 1799 to 1865. The full name index following the transcriptions of the eight registers includes the names of all agents, clerks, guardians, and free persons of color.

---

[1] Sperry, Kip, *Reading Early American Handwriting*. Genealogical Publishing Company, Inc., Baltimore, Maryland, Sixth Printing, 2008.

Many thanks are offered the very helpful and knowledgeable staff of the Georgia Department of Archives and History for their kind assistance and suggestions. Thanks also are offered Joe Garonzik of the Genealogical Publishing Company for his professional advice and counsel. Special thanks are due Marcia Tremonti for her patience and encouragement through this challenging, but interesting endeavor.

Georgia Laws

The following presents a synopsis of the various Georgia laws governing slave manumissions and registration of free persons of color prior to 1837. The synopsis is not a comprehensive list of all of the provisions of all of the laws passed at different times, but rather is intended only to be a summary of the applicable laws. Researchers desiring a more detailed discussion of the laws should consult the work of W. McDowell Rogers.[2]

On December 5, 1801, Georgia enacted a law governing the manumission of slaves.[3] In part, the act provided

> 47. Sec. I. From and after the passing of this act, it shall not be lawful for any person or persons to manumit or set free any negro slave or slaves, any mulatto, mestizo, or any other person or persons of color, who may be deemed slaves at the time of the passing of this act, in any other manner or form, than by an application to the legislature for that purpose.

The Act of December 15, 1810 required all free persons of color to register.[4]

> 56. Sec. VII. The judge of the superior or the justices of the inferior courts of the respective counties of this State, shall, upon the written application of any free negro or person of color, made at any regular term of the said courts, praying that a white person resident of the county in which such application may be made, and in which such free person of color shall reside, may be appointed his or her guardian, appoint such white person the guardian of such free person of color. And the said guardian of such free negro or person of color, shall be, and is hereby vested with all the powers and authority of guardians for the management of the persons and estates of infants; and all suits necessary to be brought for or against such free person of color, shall be in the name of such guardian, in his capacity of guardian: Provided nevertheless, that the property of such guardian shall in no case be liable for the acts or debts of his ward.

> 57. Sec. VIII. The said judges of the superior or justices of the inferior courts shall at their discretion require security from such guardian as may be appointed, for the proper management of the affairs of his ward. And such guardian shall be allowed the same compensation for the discharge of his duties as guardian, as is allowed the guardians of infants by the laws of this State.

On December 19, 1818, the legislature effectively replaced the Act of 1801.[5]

---

[2] Rogers, W. McDowell, *Free Negro Legislation in Georgia Before 1865.* The Georgia Historical Quarterly, Volume XVI, Number 1, March 1932, Page 27. Georgia Historical Society, Savannah, Georgia.

[3] Prince, Oliver H., *Digest of the Laws of the State of Georgia*, page 787. Athens, Georgia, 1837. (Hereinafter cited as Prince.)

[4] Prince, page 789.

Whereas the principles of sound policy, considered in reference to the free citizens of this State, and the exercise of humanity towards the slave population within the same, imperiously require that the number of free persons of color within this State should not be increased by manumission, or by the admission of such persons from other States to reside therein; and *whereas* divers persons of color, who are slaves by the law of this State, having never been manumitted in conformity to the same, are nevertheless in the full exercise and enjoyment of all the rights and privileges of free persons of color, without being subject to the duties and obligations incident to such persons, thereby constituting a class of people, equally dangerous to the safety of the free citizens of this State, and destructive of the comfort and happiness of the slave population thereof, which it is the duty of this legislature by all just and lawful means to suppress:

93. Sec. III. From and after the passing of this act, it shall not be lawful for any free person of color, (Indians in amity with the State, and regularly articled seamen or apprentices, arriving in any ship or vessel, excepted,) to come into this State; and each and every person or persons offending herein, shall be liable to be arrested by warrant, under the hand and seal of any magistrate in this State, and being thereof convicted in the manner hereinafter pointed out, shall be liable to a penalty not exceeding one hundred dollars, and upon failure to pay the same within the time prescribed in the sentence awarded against such person or persons, he, she, or they, shall be liable to be sold by public outcry, as a slave or slaves, in such manner as may be prescribed by the court awarding such sentence, and the proceeds of such sales shall be appropriated in the manner provided for the appropriation of penalties recovered under this act.

95. Sec. V. All and every free person or persons of color, residing or being within this State, at the time of the passing of this act, and continuing or being therein on the first day of March next, except as hereinbefore excepted, shall, on or before that day, and annually on or before the first Monday in March in each and every succeeding year, which they shall continue to be within the limits of this State, make application to the clerk of the inferior court in the county in which they reside, and it shall be the duty of said clerk to make a registry of such free person or persons of color, in a book by him to be kept for that purpose, particularly describing therein the names, ages, places of nativity and residence, time of coming into this State, and occupation or pursuit of such free person or persons of color; and such clerk shall be entitled to demand and receive fifty cents for each and every person or persons so registered as aforesaid, and for granting a certificate thereof, which he shall in like manner be bound to do so on or before the first Monday in May thereafter, if no person shall appear to gainsay the same; and to the intent that all persons concerned or interested therein, may have due notice thereof, it shall be the duty of such clerk forthwith, after the said first Monday in March in each and every year, to cause to be published in one or more of the public gazettes of the county, or in counties where there are no gazettes, in some one or more of the gazettes of the State, a list of such free persons of color,

---

[5] Prince, page 794.

4

applying for registry, with notice that certificates will be granted to such applicants, if no objections are made thereto, on or before the second Monday in April thereafter; and each and every person desirous of objecting thereto, shall file such his objections in the office of such clerk within the time specified in such notice, which proceedings shall be by the said clerk notified to the justices of the inferior court of such county, and shall be tried and determined in the manner hereinafter pointed out; and the said clerk shall grant or withhold such certificate, according to the determination thereof: *Provided*, that the expense of such publication shall be defrayed out of the county funds, where the moiety of the several penalties prescribed by this act is appropriated to the county, and out of the funds of the city of Savannah where such moiety is appropriated to the corporation of the city.

96. Sec. VI. All and every person of color (Indians in amity with this State, or regularly articled seamen or apprentices arriving in any ship or vessel excepted) who shall, after the first Monday in May next, be found within the limits of this State, whose names shall not be enrolled in the book of registry, described in the preceding section, or having been enrolled, who shall have been refused certificates in the manner therein prescribed, and who shall be working at large, enjoying the profits of his or her labor, and not in the employment of a master or owner, or of some white person, by and in virtue of an actual and bona fide contract, with the master or owner of such person of color, securing to such master or owner the profits arising from the labor of such person of color, shall be deemed, held, and taken to be slaves, and may be arrested by warrant under the hand of any magistrate of this State, and such proceedings being had as are hereinafter provided, shall be sold by public outcry as slaves, and the proceeds of such sales shall be appropriated in the manner specified in the first section of this act.

On December 22, 1819, the legislature amended the Act passed the previous year.[6]

103. Sec. I. All free persons of color contemplated in the above-recited act, who failed to comply with the provisions therein contained, shall be, and they are hereby declared to be exonerated, released, and discharged from all pains or forfeitures to which they were thereby subjected; *Provided*, they do on or before the first Monday in July next, and annually thereafter on the first Monday in July, comply with the provisions contained in said act; *Provided*, that this act shall not extend to any case where there has been an actual forfeiture and sale.

106. Sec. IV. The above-recited act shall not extend to and operate upon free persons of color who are minors, and bound out according to law.

On December 20, 1824, Georgia passed *An Act to repeal all laws and parts of laws which authorize the selling into slavery of free persons of color.*[7]

---

[6] Prince, page 799.

On December 26, 1826, the legislature passed an act amending several provisions concerning free persons of color.[8]

> 113. Sec. II. Previous to the granting of certificates of registry of freedom, it shall be the duty of the clerks of the superior and inferior courts of the several counties of this State to give ten days' notice in one of the public gazettes, or in some other public manner, of the name of the applicant or applicants, his age, &c., and of his, or hers, or their guardian or guardians.

> 114. Sec. III. Such certificate of registry of freedom, when issued as aforesaid, shall contain an accurate description of the person, age, or occupation, and residence of such person of color, and that the clerk so issuing the same shall be entitled to have and receive from the guardian of such person of color the sum of five dollars; and should any free negro or person of color transfer his or her certificate of registry of freedom obtained as aforesaid to any slave, or free negro, or other person of color, such free negro or person of color so offending shall be punished by such fine, imprisonment, and other corporal punishment as any court competent to try slaves and free persons of color may in its discretion think proper to inflict.

On December 21, 1829, Georgia passed *An Act to amend the Acts concerning the Guardianship of Free Persons of Color.*[9]

> 120. Whereas, it frequently happens that the citizens of this State decline a permanent guardianship of free persons of color, by which the ends of justice are prevented;
> *Be it enacted, &c.* That from and after the passage of this act, free persons of color may exercise the right heretofore secured to them, of suing and being sued, pleading and being impleaded, answering and being answered unto, by the aid of a next friend as well as by a guardian.

> 121. Sec. II. Guardians of free persons of color shall have the privilege, with the consent of the inferior courts, of resigning their appointments at any time they wish to do so.

On December 26, 1835, the Georgia legislature passed *An Act to amend the several laws now in force in relation to Slaves and Free Persons of Color.*[10]

> 163. Sec. I. *Be it enacted,* That from and after the passing of this act, it shall not be lawful for the clerk of any county in this State to register as free persons of

---

[7] Prince, page 800.

[8] Prince, page 800.

[9] Prince, page 802.

[10] Prince, page 810.

color, or to grant a certificate of such registry to any person of color, who shall not establish by proof, to the satisfaction of the inferior court of said county, that he or she, applying so to be registered, is *bona fide* and truly a free person of color, according to and under the laws of this State, or has been registered in this State, or has exercised all the privileges of a free person of color, for five years before the passing of this act. That it shall be the duty of such clerk to file in his office the evidence on which he shall grant such application, and that any clerk violating this law shall be guilty of a high misdemeanor, and on conviction shall be subject to a fine of three hundred dollars, to be paid one half to the informer, the other half to county purposes.

164. Sec. II. From and after the first day of June next, it shall not be lawful for any person of color, other than a slave, or a free person of color duly admitted to register in manner aforesaid, to remain in this State; and if any free person of color, other than as aforesaid, shall be found in this State after the said first day of June next, he or she shall be arrested and tried, and if convicted of a violation of this law, he or she shall pay a fine of $100, and in default of such payment, it shall be lawful for the court to bind them out as laborers until the fine is paid by the hire of such labor, and shall moreover be liable and subject to a repetition of such conviction, fine and punishment, at the end of thirty days after any such conviction and payment of such fine, until he or she shall actually depart this State, and that it shall be the duty of such [each] and every civil officer of this State to carry into effect his law.

165. Sec. III. From and after the passage of his law, it shall not be lawful for any free person of color who shall leave this State, other than to go to an adjoining State, again to return to it; and any and every free person of color entitled under the laws of this State to registry, who shall after the passage of this law go out of this State to any place other than to an adjoining State, for a temporary or other purpose, he or she, so leaving this State, shall thereby forfeit and lose his or her rights to registry as aforesaid, and all rights to reside in this State, and if thereafter found in this State, he or she shall be dealt with and subject to the pains and penalties described in the second section of this act.

170. Sec. VIII. The inferior courts of the several counties in this State shall have power and discretion to refuse and deny to any free person of color of bad character the right to register his or her name; and such free person of color shall then, after such refusal, be deemed and held a free person of color in this State in violation of this law, and be liable and subject to the pains and penalties herein prescribed.

Manumissions

Because the official policy of Georgia was to discourage and limit manumissions, the state legislature issued very few during the ante bellum period. The following acts of the legislature manumitting slaves, from 1798 through 1865, are from the database of legislative acts available on the Georgia Department of Archives and History website. Because the database, while substantial, is not complete, some additional acts of manumission may be missed. Supplemental information concerning the manumissions, including the original petitions, could survive in the State legislative records held by the archives. The full titles of the acts appear in italics.

Acts of the General Assembly of the State of Georgia: Passed at Louisville, in January and February, 1799. Vol. 1, Page 148. Sequential Number: 035.

An act to manumit and exempt from certain penalties, Silvia, and her son David, now the property of Joseph Gabriel Posner.

WHEREAS Joseph Gabriel Posner, hath by his petition presented to this present General Assembly, prayed that Silvia, a woman of color, and David her son, the property of the said Joseph Gabriel Posner, should be manumitted and discharged from slavery:

Sec. 1. Be it enacted by the Senate and House of Representatives of the State of Georgia, in General Assembly met, That from and after the passing of this act the said Silvia and David shall be and they are hereby declared to be manumitted and made free, and be thereafter utterly, clearly and fully discharged from slavery, as if the said Silvia and David had been born free.

Sec. 2. And be it further enacted, That if it shall so happen that the said Silvia or David should be charged or accused of any offence or crime whatsoever, the said Silvia or David shall be tried for such offence, in the same manner, and be entitled to the same defense, in the courts of this state, as allowed to free white persons in like cases.

Approval Date: Assented to February 9, 1799.

Acts of the General Assembly of the State of Georgia: Passed at Louisville, in January and February, 1799. Vol. 1, Page: 23. Sequential Number: 049

Acts of the General Assembly of the State of Georgia: Passed at Louisville, in November and December, 1799. Augusta: Printed by John E. Smith, Printer to the State. MDCCC.

An Act to manumit certain persons therein named.

Whereas James King, late of the city of Charleston, deceased, did by his last will and testament, bearing date the twenty-sixth day of March, in the year of our Lord one thousand seven hundred and ninety-seven, direct his executors therein named "to take care of and manumit, as soon as possible, his two negroes Lewis and China."

8

And Whereas Alexander King and Joshua Moore, the executors named in the said last will and testament of the said James King, have by petition applied to the present legislature, praying that the benevolent intentions of the said James King towards the said negroes be carried into effect:

Sec. 1. Be it therefore enacted by the Senate and House of Representatives of the State of Georgia in General Assembly met, That the said negroes Lewis and China be, and they are hereby manumitted and made free, and they are hereby entitled to the same privileges and immunities as if they had been born free.

And Whereas Ezekiel Hudnall has by his petition prayed the legislature to manumit the following slaves: Bridget Waters and her children, Leviny, Nancy, Daniel, and Syrus.

Sec. 2. Be it enacted, That the said Bridget, Leviny, Nancy, Daniel, and Syrus shall be, and they are hereby declared to be free and manumitted according to the prayer of the said petition.

And Whereas it appears to this present general assembly that a certain Harry M'Clendon, formerly the property of Jacob M'Clendon, and Rose his wife, formerly the property of Andrew M'Lean, have purchased their freedom, together with the freedom of their children, of and from their former owners, and have prayed that their freedom, as purchased, be secured by law.

Sec. 3. Be it further enacted, That the said Harry, Rose and their children Betsy and Kesiah, be and they are hereby declared to be free.

Sec. 4. Provided always, and be it further enacted, That nothing in this act contained shall be construed to give any person herein manumitted, any privileges except such as free people of color are entitled to by the laws of this state.

Approval Date: Assented to December 5, 1799.

Acts of the General Assembly of the State of Georgia Passed at Louisville, in November and December, 1801. Vol. 1, Page 40. Sequential Number: 015.

An Act to manumit and make free certain persons of colour, whose names are therein mentioned.

Whereas Richard Meriwether, and others, have petitioned the present Legislature, praying that, an Act may be passed, to manumit and make free Lucy Barrot, and Betty Barrot, Jim, commonly called Jim Lary, and a mulatto girl, named Nancy, late the property of Alexander Kevan, persons of colour, who are their right and property.

Sec. 1. Be it therefore enacted by the Senate and House of Representatives of the State of Georgia, in General Assembly met, and by the authority of the same, That Lucy Barrot, and Betty Barrot, Jim, commonly called Jim Lary, late the property of John B. Lary, and mulatto girl named Nancy, late the property of Alexander Kevan, persons of colour, be and they are hereby manumitted, and made free, and entitled to the same rights, privileges and immunities, as if they were born free.

Sec. 2. Be it further enacted, That this Act, shall not be so construed as to give, or grant unto the aforesaid Lucy Barrot, and Betty Barrot, Jim, commonly called Jim Lary, late the property of

John B. Lary, and a mulatto girl named Nancy, late the property of Alexander Kevan, persons of colour, who do appertain to the household of Richard Meriwether, and others and who are hereby manumitted and made free, any rights, privileges, or immunities, except such as free people of colour, are entitled to by the laws of this state.

Sec. 3. And be it further enacted by the authority aforesaid, That the aforesaid persons of colour, who are hereby manumitted and made free, shall nevertheless be subject and liable to any legal demands which now doth exist, against the aforesaid Richard Meriwether, and others.

Approval Date: Assented to December 1, 1801.

Acts of the General Assembly of the State of Georgia Passed in Milledgeville at an Annual Session, in November and December, 1831. Vol. 1, Page: 225. Sequential Number: 174.

An Act to be entitled an act to manumit and set free from slavery Sophia, a person of colour, the property of Eli Fenn, and to give her a name.

Be it enacted by the Senate and House of Representatives of the State of Georgia, in General Assembly met, and it is hereby enacted by the authority of the same, That from and after the passage of this act, Sophia, a person of colour, now the property of Eli Fenn, shall be manumitted and set free from slavery, and shall be entitled to all the rights, immunities, and privileges, as though she had been born free.

Sec. 2. And be it further enacted by the authority aforesaid, That in future the said Sophia shall be called and known by the name of Sophia Fenn.

Approval Date: Assented to Dec. 19, 1831.

Acts of the General Assembly of the State of Georgia Passed in Milledgeville at an Annual Session, in November and December, 1833. Vol. 1 -- Page: 289. Sequential Number: 133.

An Act to manumit and set free Mary, a woman of colour, and her child Cordelia, now the property, wife and child of Lovewell C. Fluellin, a free man of colour.

Be it enacted by the Senate and House of Representatives of the State of Georgia, in General Assembly met, and it is hereby enacted by authority of the same, That from and after the passing of this act, Mary, a woman of colour, and her child Cordelia, now the property, wife and child, of Lovewell C. Fluellin, a free man of colour, shall be manumitted and set free, from slavery, and shall be entitled to all the rights, immunities, and privileges, as though she and her child Cordelia had been born free.

Approval Date: Assented to 24th Dec. 1833.

Acts of the General Assembly of the State of Georgia Passed in Milledgeville at an Annual Session, in November and December, 1834. Vol. 1, Page: 230. Sequential Number: 173.

An Act to manumit and set free certain persons therein mentioned.

10

Sec. 1. Be it enacted by the Senate and House of Representatives of the State of Georgia in General Assembly met, That from and after the passage of this act, Fanny Hickman, who is, and has been for more than thirty years, the wife of Paschal Hickman of the county of Burke, shall be, and she is hereby declared to be free, and entitled to all the privileges and immunities appertaining to free persons of colour generally in this State.

And whereas the said Paschal Hickman since his intermarriage with his said wife Fanny has had several children, and whereas by the laws of this State the said children follow the condition of their mother.

Sec. 2. Be it therefore enacted by the Senate and House of Representatives of the State of Georgia in General Assembly met, That all said children heretofore born, -- to wit, John, Grove, Henry, William, Hetty, Eliza, and Frank, -- by and in consequence of said intermarriage between the said Paschal Hickman and Fanny his wife, shall be, and they are hereby declared to be free, and placed on the same footing that free persons of colour are usually placed in this State, and entitled to inherit from the said Paschal, as their father, any property which by the laws of this State would go to his children should he die without a will.

Approval Date: Assented to Dec. 22d, 1834.

Acts of the General Assembly of the State of Georgia, passed in Milledgeville, at a Biennial Session, in November, December, January, February & March, 1855-56. Compiled, and notes added, by John W. Duncan.

Part II. Local and Private Laws, Title XXV. Slaves. 1855 Vol. 1, Page: 539. Sequential Number: 537, Law Number: No. 534.

An Act to manumit a negro man slave, named Boston, the property of E. B. Way, Catharine P. Wheeler, Thomas B. Wheeler, H. R. Wheeler, and Eugene Bacon of the State of Georgia, and county of Liberty, and John Savage of the county of Chatham, and State aforesaid.

Whereas, during a long life, the negro man slave, named Boston, has served his owners with uniform fidelity, and whereas, during the war of 1812, he served with his master in the company from Liberty county, which marched to Darien, and remained there under arms in momentary expectation of an engagement with the British who threatened a landing, and other important services to the public.

Sec. I. Be it therefore enacted &c., That in consideration of the services stated in the foregoing preamble, and the petition accompanying this bill, the negro, man slave Boston, the property of E. B Way, Catharine P. Wheeler, Thomas B. Wheeler, H. R. Wheeler, and Eugene Bacon the of county of Liberty, and State aforesaid, and John Savage of the county of Chatham, and State aforesaid, said owners all consenting thereto, be and he is hereby manumitted and forever set free, and shall hereafter enjoy all the rights and privileges to which free negroes in the State of Georgia are entitled.

Approval Date: March 6th, 1856.

Assented to December 22d, 1834.

Acts of the General Assembly of the State of Georgia, passed at Milledgeville, at an Annual Session, in November and December, 1822. Vol. 1, Page: 83. Sequential Number: 080.

An Act to carry into effect the last will and testament of James Robinson late of Greene county, deceased, and to emancipate a female slave by the name of Rachel.

Whereas, the said James Robinson, prior to his death, made a will, containing a clause, among other things, emancipating a female slave by the name of Rachel, the property of him the said James; and whereas the said James, required his executors, to carry this clause of his will into execution, by procuring a legislative act to legalize the same; and the said female slave being desirous of removing to her native state, Maryland:

Sec. 1. Be it therefore enacted by the Senate and House of Representatives of the State of Georgia in General Assembly met, and it is hereby enacted by the authority of the same, That from the passage of this act, the said female slave Rachel, be, and she is hereby fully and completely emancipated and set free according to the intent and meaning of the will of him, the said James Robinson: Provided, that said negro Rachel be, and she is hereby liable to all the fines, penalties and privileges, now imposed and allowed in this state to free people of colour. Provided always that the said Rachel shall not be entitled to the benefits of this act if found in this state within one year after the passing of this act.

Approval Date: Assented to December 21, 1822.

Acts of the General Assembly of the State of Georgia, passed at Milledgeville, at an Annual Session, in November and December, 1823. Vol. 1, Page: 146. Sequential Number: 113.

An Act to carry into effect the last will and testament of James Robinson, late of Greene county, deceased, so far as to manumit a female slave by the name of Chloe.

Whereas, James Robinson, late of Greene county, deceased, previous to his death, did duly make and publish his last will and testament, containing among other things, a clause emancipating a female slave by the name of Chloe, the property of him the said James -- And whereas, the said James required his executors to carry this clause of his said will into execution, by procuring a legislative act to legalize the same.

Sec. 1. Be it therefore enacted by the Senate and House of Representatives of the State of Georgia, in General Assembly met, and it is hereby enacted by the authority of the same, That from and after the passage of this act, the said female slave Chloe be, and she is hereby fully and completely emancipated and set free, according to the true intent and meaning of him the said James Robinson: Provided, That the said negro Chloe be, and she is hereby liable to all the fines, penalties and privileges, now imposed on, and allowed to, free people of color in this state.

Approval Date: Assented to Nov. 24, 1823.

Acts of the General Assembly of the State of Georgia, passed in Milledgeville at an Annual Session in October, November, and December 1830. Vol. 1, Page: 187. Sequential Number: 137.

An Act to emancipate and set free, Joy, Rose and her two sons Jim and John, formerly the property of Ramond Demere, late of St. Simon's Island, in the county of Glynn.

Sec. 1. Be it enacted by the Senate and House of Representatives of the State of Georgia, in General Assembly met, and it is hereby enacted by the authority of the same, That from and after the passage of this act, Joy, Rose and her two sons, Jim and John, formerly the property of Ramond Demere, late of St. Simon's Island, in the county of Glynn, be, and they are hereby emancipated and set free, as an acknowledgment of their extraordinary services in protecting the property of their owner, Ramond Demere of St. Simon's Island, from the depredations of the British Maurauders during the late war with Great Britain: Provided, That the Executors and heirs of the said Demere shall be held liable for the support and maintenance of said slaves, so far as to indemnify the county of Glynn or any other county against all damage by occasion of their infirmity and inability to support themselves.

Sec. 2. And be it further enacted, That the said Joy, Rose and her two sons, Jim and John, be, and they are hereby entitled to all the privileges, and subject to all the laws of this State, for the regulation and Government of free persons of colour.

Approval Date: Assented to December 23d 1830.

Acts of the General Assembly of the State of Georgia, passed in Milledgeville, at an Annual Session in November and December 1834. Vol. 1, Page: 229. Sequential Number: 172.

An Act to emancipate Sam, a negro slave.

Whereas, by a concurred resolution of both branches of the General Assembly of this State, passed at the last session of the Legislature, the Governor of this State, in consideration of the important services rendered by Sam, a negro man slave, in extinguishing the fire on the State-house, was authorized and required to purchase said negro Sam of his owner for the purpose of his emancipation; and his purchase having been effected.

Sec. 1. Be it therefore enacted by the Senate and House of Representatives of the State of Georgia in General Assembly met, and it is hereby enacted by the authority of the same, That from and immediately after the passage of this act, said negro man Sam, formerly the property of John Marler, be, and he is hereby emancipated and set free; and that he enjoy all the privileges and immunities given by the laws of this State to free persons of colour in such manner as if he were born free, -- any law to the contrary notwithstanding.

Approval Date: Assented to 20th December, 1834.

Acts of the General Assembly of the State of Georgia, passed in Milledgeville, at an Annual Session in November and December 1834. Vol. 1 -- Page: 231. Sequential Number: 174.

An Act to emancipate Patsy and Cyrus, the wife and father of Solomon Humphries, a free person of colour; and Edmund, late the property of Theophilus Hill's estate, of Oglethorpe county.

Whereas, Solomon Humphries, a free person of colour, has paid to the former owners of Patsy and Cyrus, his wife and father, the price asked for them.

Sec. 1. Be it therefore enacted by the Senate and House of Representatives of the State of Georgia in General Assembly met, and it is hereby enacted by the authority of the same, That from and immediately after the passing of this act, the said Patsy and Cyrus, the wife and father of Solomon Humphries, and Edmund, late the property of Theophilus Hill's estate, of Oglethorpe county, shall be emancipated and set free, and shall be entitled to all the rights, immunities, and privileges of free persons of colour, as though they had been born free.

Approval Date: Assented to 20th Dec. 1834.

In addition to the manumissions, the legislature enacted laws concerning three separate free persons of color.

Acts of the General Assembly of the State of Georgia: Passed at Milledgeville, at an Extra Session, in April and May, 1821. Volume I – Page: 20. Sequential Number: 109.

An Act for the relief of Austin, otherwise called Austin Dabney, a Freeman of colour.

Whereas, by an act of the General Assembly of the state of Georgia, passed on the fourteenth day of August, 1786, it is stated that the said Austin, during the Revolution, instead of advantaging himself of the times to withdraw from the American lines and enter with the majority of his color and fellow-slaves in the service of his Britannic Majesty, and his officers and vassals, did voluntarily enroll himself in some one of the corps under the command of Col. Elijah Clark, and in several actions and engagements behaved against the common enemy with a bravery and fortitude which would have honored a freeman; and in one of which engagements he was severely wounded and rendered incapable of hard servitude; and policy as well as gratitude, demand a return for such services and behavior from the Commonwealth; and it was further stated in said act, that said Austin "should be entitled to the annuity allowed by this state, to wounded and disabled soldiers." And the said Austin having petitioned the Legislature for some aid in his declining years, and this body considering him an object entitled to the attention and gratitude of the state he has defended, and in whose service he has been disabled;

Sec. 1. Be it enacted by the Senate and House of Representatives in General Assembly met, and it is hereby enacted by the same, That the lot or fraction of land situate, lying and being in the county of Walton, in the first district, and known and distinguished by number two hundred and eighty four, containing one hundred and twelve acres, be the same more or less, be and the same hereby is conveyed and transferred to the said Austin during the period of the natural life of him the said Austin Dabney.

Sec. 2. And be it further enacted, That the Austin Dabney be, and is hereby entitled to a plat for the same.

Sec. 3. And be it further enacted, That the lot and number above named is, and shall be exempted from the contemplated sale of Fractions in said county, authorized by an act at the annual session of the Legislature, in the year 1820.

Assented to, 16th May, 1821.

14

Acts of the General Assembly of the State of Georgia: Passed in Milledgeville, at a Biennial Session, in November, December, January, February & March, 1855-56. Compiled, and Notes Added, by John W. Duncan. Part II – Local and Private Laws. Title XXV. Slaves. 1855. Volume I – Page: 539. Sequential Number: 536. Law Number: 533.

An Act to exempt Daniel and Lucinda his wife, the property of Harrison W. Riley, nominal slaves from the tax now imposed by law on nominal slaves.

3. Sec. 1. Be it enacted, &c., That Daniel, the property of Harrison W. Riley, and Lucinda, the wife of said Daniel, nominal slaves, be exempt from the tax now imposed by law on nominal slaves, and that they be required to pay only such tax as now required by law from free persons of color.

Approved, March 5th, 1856.

Acts of the General Assembly of the State of Georgia: Passed in Milledgeville, at an Annual Session, in November and December, 1862. Title IX. Slaves and Free Persons of Color. Volume I. Sequential Number: 101.

An Act to authorize Jane Miller, a free person of color, to sell herself into perpetual slavery.

1. Sec. 1. Be it enacted &c., That Jane Miller, a free person of color, in Clarke county be, and she is hereby authorized to voluntarily become the slave of E. S. Sims for life.

2. Sec. II. That in order to carry into effect the first section of this Act, the said E. S. Sims and the said Jane Miller, shall go before the Justices of the Inferior Court, or a majority of them, in said county, who shall faithfully and fully examine her as to her willingness to become the slave for life of said E. S. Sone; and upon being satisfied of the same, they shall pass an order to the effect that the said Jane Miller be held, deemed and considered he slave of the said E. S. Sims for and during her natural life, subject to all the incidents of slavery, except the liability of being sold during the lifetime of said Sims, by himself, or his creditors for his debts; he sole consideration for which voluntary enslavement on her part, shall be the obligation thereby incurred by her master of feeding, clothing and protecting her.

3. Sec III. It shall be the duty of the Clerk of he Inferior Court to record said order on he minutes of the Court as evidence of title; also to record the same in the book kept by him for recording other evidences of tittle to property; for which the said E. S. Sims shall pay to said Clerk a fee of five dollars.

Assented to December 9th, 1862.

Appling County

The Genealogical Society of Salt Lake City, Utah microfilmed the original record book held by the Superior Court in the courthouse at Baxley, Georgia. A copy is available in the microfilm reading room of the Georgia Department of Archives and History in Morrow, Georgia. The heading on the microfilm roll reads

Appling County
State of Georgia
Inferior Court
Registration of Free Persons of Color
1843-1856

At the top of the first page, the clerk wrote

> H. Nunez & J. Harman & A. Harman Appl for R for 1847 this day.

Just below that notation, the clerk wrote

Record Book for
Guardian & Executrs
Book A, 1873

149 J. Simmons
Return

In spite of the apparent title, the clerk entered the registration of free persons of color in a short paragraph format. The following is a full transcription of the first registration.

> Georgia   } Personally came Abraham Harmons a native borned of
> Appling County   } Richmond County in the State aforesaid, where he
> remained until arrived at the age of twenty one years old. Then went to Liberty County. Then went to Appling, Both of said State, wher he now registers himself in Conformity to the law as a free person of Color, about thirty fore years old, a farmer by occupation.
>
> Also his wife, Selah Harmans, who was borned in the County of Hancock in the State aforesaid, aged about thirty years old, who lives of course in the occupancy of house wifery with her husband Abraham Harmans as above registered. This 20th December 1843. Jesse Mobley, Clerk

The following table presents the relevant information from the registry in a standard format.

Name	Age	Nativity	Residence	Occupation	Date
Abraham Harmons	34	Born in Richmond County	When 21 years old, went to Liberty County, then to Appling County.	Farmer	20 Dec 1843
Selah Harmons, wife of Abraham	30	Born in Hancock County		House wifery	20 Dec 1843
John H. Harmon	27	Born in Liberty County	When 21 years old went to Bibb County, then to Ware County, then to Appling County.	Farmer	20 Dec 1843
John P. Harmon	21	Born in Roberson County, North Carolina	When 12 years old went to Twiggs County, then to Laurence County, then to Appling County.	Farmer	20 Dec 1843
William Jones	48	Born in Jefferson County	When small went to Richmond County. When 6 or 7 years old went to Burke County, then to Columbia County, then to Emanuel County, then to Appling County.	Farmer	20 Dec 1843
Hugh E. Nunez	53	Born in Jefferson County	Went to Tattnall County, then to Appling County.	Farmer	20 Dec 1843
Daniel Nunez	47	Born in Jefferson County	Went to Tattnall County, then to Ware County, then to Camden County, then to	Farmer	20 Dec 1843

17

Name	Age	Nativity	Residence	Occupation	Date
			Appling County.		
William Nail	21	Born in Tattnall County	Moved to Appling County	Farmer	20 Dec 1843
Leroy Nail	22	Born in Tattnall County	Moved to Appling County	Farmer	20 Dec 1843
Leroy Nail	23	Born in Tattnall County	Moved to Appling County	Farmer	20 Jun 1844
William Nail	22	Born in Tattnall County	Moved to Appling County	Farmer	20 Jun 1844
Abraham Harmon	37	Born in Richmond County	When 21 years old, went to Liberty County, then to Appling County.	Farmer	28 Mar 1846
Francis Harmon	31	Born in Richmond County	Moved to Bibb County, then to Appling County	Farmer	29 May 1846
Hugh Nunez	56	Born in Jefferson County	Went to Tattnall County, then to Appling County.	Farmer	21 Dec 1846
Daniel Nunez	50	Born in Jefferson County	Went to Tattnall County, then to Ware County, then to Camden County, then to Appling County.	Farmer	21 Dec 1846
Hugh Nunez	57	Born in Jefferson County	Went to Tattnall County, then to Appling County.	Farmer	20 Dec 1847
Daniel Nunez	51	Born in Jefferson	Went to Tattnall County, then to	Farmer	20 Dec

Name	Age	Nativity	Residence	Occupation	Date
		County	Ware County, then to Camden County, then to Appling County.		1847
Abraham Harmon	38	Born in Richmond County	Moved to Liberty County, then to Appling County.	Farmer	20 Dec 1847
Francis Harmon	31	Born in Richmond County	Moved to Bibb County, then to Appling County	Farmer	20 Dec 1847
John Harmon		Born in Richmond County	Moved to Appling County	Farmer	20 Dec 1847
William Nail	24	Born in Tattnall County	Moved to Appling County	Farmer	20 Dec 1847
Leroy Nail	27	Born in Tattnall County	Moved to Appling County	Farmer	20 Dec 1847
Benjamin Cousins	35	Born in Augusta	Moved to Milledgeville, then to Macon, then to Appling County	Farmer	20 Dec 1847
Hughes Eunice	38	Born in Jefferson County	Moved to Tattnall County, then to Appling County	Farmer	21 Dec 1848
Daniel Eunice	52	Born in Jefferson County	Moved to Tattnall County, then to Ware County, then to Camden County, then to Appling County	Farmer	21 Dec 1848
Abraham Harmon	39	Born in Richmond	Moved to Liberty County, then to	Farmer	21 Dec

Name	Age	Nativity	Residence	Occupation	Date
		County	Appling County.		1848
William Nail	25	Born in Tattnall County	Moved to Appling County	Farmer	21 Dec 1848
Leroy Nail	28	Born in Tattnall County	Moved to Appling County	Farmer	21 Dec 1848
Francis Harmon	33	Born in Richmond County	Moved to Bibb County, then to Appling County	Farmer	21 Dec 1848
Hughey Eunice	38	Born in Jefferson County	Moved to Tattnall County, then to Appling County	Farmer	20 Dec 1849
Daniel Eunice	53	Born in Jefferson County	Moved to Tattnall County, then to Ware County, then to Camden County, then to Appling County	Farmer	20 Dec 1849
Abraham Harmon	40	Born in Richmond County	Moved to Liberty County, then to Appling County.	Farmer	20 Dec 1849
Francis Harmon	33	Born in Richmond County	Moved to Bibb County, then to Appling County	Farmer	20 Dec 1849
Hughey Eunice	60	Born in Jefferson County	Moved to Tattnall County, then to Appling County	Farmer	25 Dec 1850
Daniel Eunice	54	Born in Jefferson County	Moved to Tattnall County, then to Ware County, then to Camden County, then to Appling County	Farmer	25 Dec 1850
Abraham Harmon	41	Born in	Moved to Liberty	Farmer	25

Name	Age	Nativity	Residence	Occupation	Date
		Richmond County	County, then to Appling County.		Dec 1850
Francis Harmon	34	Born in Richmond County	Moved to Bibb County, then to Appling County	Farmer	25 Dec 1850
John Harmon		Born in Richmond County	Moved to Appling County	Farmer	25 Dec 1850
William Nail	27	Born in Tattnall County	Moved to Appling County	Farmer	25 Dec 1850
Leroy Nail	30	Born in Tattnall County	Moved to Appling County	Farmer	25 Dec 1850
Hughey Eunice	61	Born in Jefferson County	Moved to Tattnall County, then to Appling County	Farmer	20 Dec 1851
Daniel Eunice	55	Born in Jefferson County	Moved to Tattnall County, then to Ware County, then to Camden County, then to Appling County	Farmer	20 Dec 1851
Abraham Harmon	42	Born in Richmond County	Moved to Liberty County, then to Appling County.	Farmer	20 Dec 1851
Francis Harmon	35	Born in Richmond County	Moved to Bibb County, then to Appling County	Farmer	20 Dec 1851
John Harmon		Born in Richmond County	Moved to Appling County	Farmer	20 Dec 1851
William Nail	28	Born in Tattnall County	Moved to Appling County	Farmer	20 Dec 1851

Name	Age	Nativity	Residence	Occupation	Date
Leroy Nail	31	Born in Tattnall County	Moved to Appling County	Farmer	20 Dec 1851
John Horn	21	Born in Telfair County	Moved to Appling County	Farmer	1850 20 Dec 1851
Abraham Harmon	43	Born in Richmond County	Moved to Liberty County, then to Appling County.	Farmer	20 Jan 1852
William Nail	29	Born in Tattnall County	Moved to Appling County	Farmer	20 Jan 1852
Leroy Nail	32	Born in Tattnall County	Moved to Appling County	Farmer	20 Jan 1852
John Horn	22	Born in Telfair County	Moved to Appling County	Farmer	20 Jan 1852
Abraham Harmon	44	Born in Richmond County	Moved to Liberty County, then to Appling County.	Farmer	10 Aug 1853
William Nail	30	Born in Tattnall County	Moved to Appling County	Farmer	10 Aug 1853
Leroy Nail	33	Born in Tattnall County	Moved to Appling County	Farmer	10 Aug 1853
John Horn	23	Born in Telfair County	Moved to Appling County	Farmer	10 Aug 1853
William Nail	33	Born in Tattnall County	Moved to Appling County	Farmer	1 Jul 1856

Camden County

In 1958, the Genealogical Society of Salt Lake City, Utah microfilmed the original record book held by the Superior Court in the courthouse at Woodbine, Georgia. A copy is available in the microfilm reading room of the Georgia Department of Archives and History in Morrow, Georgia. The heading on the microfilm roll reads

Camden County
State of Georgia
Superior Court
Registration of Free Persons of Color1819-1843

As noted on the inside front cover, the original record book was laminated by the Georgia Department of Archives and History in 1953, the book remaining the property of the Office of the clerk of the Superior Court. At the top of the first page, the clerk wrote

> Georgia, Camden County. The following is a list of Free persons of Colour that have registered their names agreeable to an act of the Legislature of the said State passed at Milledgeville on the Nineteenth day of December Eighteen hundred and Eighteen.

The clerk entered each registration in a short paragraph. The first five entries complete the first page of the register.

> Viz.   1819
> Adam, a free man of Colour, aged about thirty years, born in East Florida, Came to the State in 1815 as a free man. Occupation, a boatman.
>
> Betty, the mother of Adam, a Free Woman of Colour, about Sixty years old, made free in he year 1815 and of no occupation, being blind.
>
> Cato, a free man of Color, aged about Sixty five years, made free by the last Will of Thomas Norris in the year ___, a carpenter by trade, residence in the town of St. Mary's ever Since that time.
>
> Belinda, a free woman of Colour, aged about Sixty five years, made free by the Will of Thomas Norris deceased in the year ___, occupation a common laborer, resided in the Town of St. Mary's ever Since that time.
>
> Sipio, A Free man of Colour, Thirty one years of age, Born Free, occupation a Boatman, formerly resided in New Orleans, and has resided in the State of Georgia in the Town of St. Mary's ever Since he came.

The transcription of the original record consists of a table of the extracted relative information presented in a standard format.

Name	Age	Nativity	When Came to Georgia	Occupation	Date
Adam	30	East Florida	1815	Boatman	1819
Betty, mother of Adam	60		Free in 1815	No Occupation. Blind	1819
Cato	65	Made free by the will of Thomas Norris	Residence in St. Mary's since freedom	Carpenter.	1819
Belinda	65		Residence in St. Mary's since freedom	Made free by the will of Thomas Norris	1819
Sipio	31		Born free. Formerly resided in New Orleans, resides St. Mary's ever since.	Boatman	1819
Wyley Brickell	25	Made free by the will of John Brickell when he was born	Principally resided in Georgia, now resides St. Mary's	Tailor	1819
Judeah	24		Formerly resided in Florida, in Georgia about 1 year	Laborer	1819
Betsey, daughter of Judeah	11	Born free in Florida	In Georgia about 1 year		1819
Andrew, son of Judeah	7	Born free in Florida	In Georgia about 1 year		1819

Name	Age	Nativity	When Came to Georgia	Occupation	Date
Elizabeth, daughter of Judeah	5	Born free in Florida	In Georgia about 1 year		1819
Emanuwell	30	Born free	Formerly resided in Portugal, Lisbon, in St. Mary's 9 years	Mariner	1819
Rivers	55	Made free in East Florida 1815	1815, now resides St. Mary's	Fisherman	1819
Mary	44	Made free by her master in East Florida	Resides St. Mary's	Laborer	1819
Polly, daughter of Mary	10	Born free in Georgia	Resides St. Mary's		1819
Willson, son of Mary	5	Born free in St. Mary's	Resides in St. Mary's		1819
William, son of Mary	5	Born free in St. Mary's	Resides in St. Mary's		1819
Norris, son of Mary	3	Born free in St. Mary's	Resides in St. Mary's		1819
Amers, daughter of Mary	1	Born free in St. Mary's	Resides in St. Mary's		1819
Fanney	30	Made free by John Aggerett in East Florida 1813	Resides in St. Mary's	Common laborer	1819
George, son of Fanney	5	Born free in St. Mary's	Resides in St. Mary's		1819

Name	Age	Nativity	When Came to Georgia	Occupation	Date
Rosaline, daughter of Fanney	3	Born free in St. Mary's	Resides in St. Mary's		1819
Remer Brunett	30	Formerly resided Charleston, South Carolina	Resides in St. Mary's for 9 years		1819
James Alfred Gaujan	16	Born free. Formerly resided Charleston, South Carolina	In Georgia 8 years, now in St. Mary's	Shopkeeper	1819
Suzett Devall	35	Born free island of Santo Domingo	In St. Mary's 15 years		1819
Jacob Mure	39	Born free in Georgia	Resided principal part of his life in St. Mary's	Laborer	1819
Thomas Mure	65	Born free in Georgia	Resided principal part of his life in Georgia, now in Camden County		1819
Pattey Tims	60	Set free by her master Mr. Tims	Resided in Camden County 12 years since her freedom	Common laborer	1819
Mariah	30	Africa	Resident of East Florida since Aug 1802, where	House servant of George J. F.	1819

Name	Age	Nativity	When Came to Georgia	Occupation	Date
			she purchased her freedom from George J. F. Clarke, Esq. Resides St. Mary's since Sept. 1817	Clarke	
Flora	40	Johns Island, South Carolina. Obtained freedom by purchase from firm Panton Leslie & Co. in East Florida 1796.	Resides in St. Mary's since June 1817	House servant of George J. F. Clarke	1819
Clement Labattre	30	Born St. Marks, Santo Domingo	Resides St. Mary's 24 years.	Sailor. Mulatto. 5 feet 7 inches tall	1819
George Adams	40	Connecticut	Resides St. Mary's 8 years	Laborer. Black. 6 feet 1½ inches tall	1819
Delia	39	Made free in East Florida 1816		House servant to Adam Cooper in Camden County	1819
William, son of Delia	19	Made free in East Florida		In employ of Adam	1819

Name	Age	Nativity	When Came to Georgia	Occupation	Date
		1816		Cooper	
Nancy, daughter of Delia	17	Made free in East Florida 1816		In employ of Adam Cooper	1819
John, son of Delia	15	Made free in East Florida 1816		In employ of Adam Cooper	1819
Hetty, daughter of Delia	13	Made free in East Florida 1816		In employ of Adam Cooper	1819
Kezia, daughter of Delia	11	Made free in East Florida 1816		In employ of Adam Cooper	1819
Esther, daughter of Delia	9	Made free in East Florida 1816		In employ of Adam Cooper	1819
Mary, daughter of Delia	7	Made free in East Florida 1816		Resides with Adam Cooper	1819
Josiah, son of Delia	5	Made free in East Florida 1816		Resides with Adam Cooper	1819
Adam	31	East Florida	1815 as a free man	Boatman	1820
Betty, mother of Adam	61	Made free in East Florida	Resides St. Mary's	No occupation. Blind	1820

Name	Age	Nativity	When Came to Georgia	Occupation	Date
		1815			
Cato	74	Made free by will of Thomas Norris	Resides St. Mary's since master's deceased	Carpenter	1820
Belinda	66	Made free by will of Thomas Norris	Resides St. Mary's	Common laborer	1820
Sipio	32	Born free New Orleans	Resides St. Mary's	Boatman. Mulatto	1820
Wyley Brickell	26	Made free by will of John Brickell	Resides in St. Mary's	Tailor	1820
Judeah	25		In Georgia 2 years, from East Florida. Resides St. Mary's	Common laborer	1820
Emanuwell	31	Formerly resided Portugal, Lisbon	Resides St. Mary's 10 years	Mariner. Mulatto	1820
Rivers	56	Made free East Florida 1815	1815, now resides St. Mary's	Fisherman	1820
Mary	43	Made free by master	Formerly resided East Florida, now St. Mary's	Common laborer	1820
John, son of Mary		Born free Camden	Since birth in St. Mary's	House carpenter	1820

Name	Age	Nativity	When Came to Georgia	Occupation	Date
		County			
Charles, son of Mary	19	Born free Camden County	Resides St. Mary's with mother	Common laborer	1820
Henry, son of Mary	13	Born free Camden County	Resides St. Mary's with mother		1820
Polly, daughter of Mary	11	Born free Camden County	Resides St. Mary's with mother		1820
Willson, son of Mary	8	Born free Camden County	Resides St. Mary's with mother		1820
William, son of Mary	6	Born free Camden County	Resides St. Mary's with mother		1820
Norris, son of Mary	4	Born free Camden County	Resides St. Mary's with mother		1820
Amey, daughter of Mary	2	Born free Camden County	Resides St. Mary's with mother		1820
Fanney	31	Made free by John Aggelett in East Florida 1813	Born in Georgia, resided in Georgia since freedom, now St. Mary's	Common laborer	1820
George, son of Fanney	6	Born free St. Mary's	Resides St. Mary's with mother		1820
Rosaline, daughter	4	Born free	Resides St.		1820

Name	Age	Nativity	When Came to Georgia	Occupation	Date
of Fanney		St. Mary's	Mary's with mother		
Remil Brunett	31	Born free, formerly resided Charleston, South Carolina	Resides St. Mary's 10 years	Merchant	1820
James Alfred Gaujan	17	Born free, formerly resided Charleston, South Carolina	Resides St. Mary's 9 years	Shopkeeper	1820
Suzett Duvall	36	Born free Santo Domingo	Resides St. Mary's 16 years	No occupation. Insane	1820
Thomas Mure	66	Born free in Georgia	Resided principal part of his life in Georgia, now Cumberland Island	Carpenter	1820
Jacob Mure	40	Born free in Georgia	Resided principal part of his life in Georgia, now St. Mary's	Common laborer	1820
Pattey Tims	61	Made free by master Mr. Tims	Resides Camden County about 13 years, since freedom	Common laborer	1820

Name	Age	Nativity	When Came to Georgia	Occupation	Date
Mariah	31	Africa	Resided East Florida since Aug 1802, in St. Mary's since Sep 1817 when she purchased her freedom from George J. F. Clarke, Esq.	House servant to George J. F. Clarke	1820
Flora	41	Johns Island, South Carolina	Purchased her freedom from firm Panton Leslie & Co. in East Florida in 1796	Since Jun 1817, house servant to George J. F. Clarke, Esq. in St. Mary's	1820
Member Norris	55		Came with owner Thomas Norris from Jamaica about 30 years ago, then sold o Charles Jackson, Esq., who emancipated her, ever since resides St. Mary's	Washer woman	1820
Clement Labatty	31	Santo Domingo	Resides St. Mary's 25 years	Mulatto. Sailor	1820
George Adams	41	Connecticut	Resides St. Mary's 9	Common laborer.	1820

Name	Age	Nativity	When Came to Georgia	Occupation	Date
			years	Black man	
Delia	40	Made free in East Florida 1816		House servant o Adam Cooper in Camden County	1820
William, son of Delia	20	Made free in East Florida 1816		In employ of Adam Cooper on farm in Camden County	1820
Nancy, daughter of Delia	18	Made free in East Florida 1816		House servant to Adam Cooper in Camden County	1820
John, son of Delia	16	Made free in East Florida 1816		Apprentice to carpenter trade in St. Mary's	1820
Hetty, daughter of Delia	14	Made free in East Florida 1816		In employ of Adam Cooper in Camden County	1820
Keziah, daughter of Delia	12	Made free in East Florida 1816		In employ of Adam Cooper in Camden County	1820
Esther, daughter of Delia	10	Made free in East Florida		In employ of Adam Cooper in Camden	1820

Name	Age	Nativity	When Came to Georgia	Occupation	Date
		1816		County	
Mary, daughter of Delia	8	Made free in East Florida 1816	Resides with Adam Cooper in Camden County		1820
Josiah, son of Delia	6	Made free in East Florida 1816	Resides with Adam Cooper in Camden County		1820
Adam	32	East Florida	1815, formerly belonged to William Gibson, Esq. Resides St. Mary's	Boatman	1821
Bettey	62	Made free by William Gibson, Esq. in East Florida	Resides with son in St. Mary's	No occupation. blind	1821
Cato Norris	67	Made free by will of Thomas Norris	Resides in St. Mary's since his freedom	Carpenter	1821
Belinda	67	Made free by will of Thomas Norris	Resides in St. Mary's since his freedom	Common laborer	1821
John Sipio	33	Born free and formerly resided in New	Resides in St. Mary's	Boatman	1821

Name	Age	Nativity	When Came to Georgia	Occupation	Date
		Orleans			
Jacob Mure	53	Born Georgia	Resided principal part of his life in Camden County	Common laborer	1821
Wyley Brickell	27	Made free by will of John Brickell when he was born	Resided principally in Georgia, now in St. Mary's	Tailor	1821
Judeah	26	Formerly resided East Florida	Resides St. Mary's	Common laborer	1821
Betsey, daughter of Judeah	13	Born free in East Florida	Resides St. Mary's with mother, 3 years		1821
Andrew, son of Judeah	9	Born free in East Florida	Resides St. Mary's with mother, 3 years		1821
Elizabeth, daughter of Judeah	7	Born free in East Florida	Resides St. Mary's with mother, 3 years		1821
Emanuwell	32	Bron free, formerly resided Portugal, Lisbon	Resides St. Mary's 11 years	Mariner. Mulatto	1821
Clement Labatte	32	Born Santo Domingo	Resides St. Mary's 26 years	Mariner. Mulatto	1821

Name	Age	Nativity	When Came to Georgia	Occupation	Date
George Adams	42	Connecticut	Resides St. Mary's 10 years	Common laborer	1821
Thomas Mure	67	Born free in Georgia	Resided principal part of his life in Georgia, now at Cumberland Island	Carpenter	1821
Member Norris	56	Came owner Thomas Norris from Jamaica, about 31 years ago	Sold o Charles Jackson, Esq. who emancipated her, ever since resided St. Mary's	Wash woman	1821
Mariah		Africa. Purchased her freedom from George J. F. Clarke, Esq. in 1796.	Formerly resided Augusta. Resided St. Mary's since 1817.	House servant to George J. F. Clarke, Esq.	1821
Flora	42	Johns Island, South Carolina.	Purchased her freedom from firm Panton Laslie & Co. in 1796. Resides St. Mary's since 1817.	House servant to George J. F. Clarke, Esq.	1821
Suzett Duvall	37	Born free Santo Domingo	Resides St. Mary's 17 years	No occupation. Insane	1821

Name	Age	Nativity	When Came to Georgia	Occupation	Date
James Alfred Garjan	18	Born free	Formerly resided Charleston, South Carolina, in St. Mary's 10 years	Shopkeeper	1821
Remil Burnett	32	Born free	Formerly resided Charleston, South Carolina, now resides 11 years	Merchant	1821
Fanney	32	Born Georgia. Made free by John Aggarett in East Florida 1813.	Resided principal part of her life in St. Mary's	Common laborer	1821
George, son of Fanney	7	Born free in St. Mary's	Resides with mother		1821
Rosaline	5	Born free in St. Mary's	Resides with mother		1821
Mary	41	Made free by her master	Formerly resided East Florida, now resides St. Mary's	Common laborer	1821
Sipio, son of Mary	21	Born Camden County	Resided in Camden County since birth, now resides St. Mary's	House carpenter	1821

Name	Age	Nativity	When Came to Georgia	Occupation	Date
Charles, son of Mary	20	Born Camden County	Resides St. Mary's	Common laborer	1821
Henry, son of Mary	14	Born Camden County	Resides St. Mary's with his mother		1821
Polly, daughter of Mary	12	Born Camden County	Resides St. Mary's with his mother		1821
Willson, son of Mary	9	Born Camden County	Resides St. Mary's with his mother		1821
William, son of Mary	7	Born Camden County	Resides St. Mary's with his mother		1821
Norris, son of Mary	5	Born Camden County	Resides St. Mary's with his mother		1821
Amey, daughter of Mary	3	Born Camden County	Resides St. Mary's with his mother		1821
John, son of Mary	10 mos	Born Camden County	Resides St. Mary's with his mother		1821
Delia	41	Made free in East Florida 1816		House servant to Adam Cooper in Camden County	1821
William, son of Delia	21	Made free in East Florida 1816		In employ of Adam Cooper on farm in Camden	1821

Name	Age	Nativity	When Came to Georgia	Occupation	Date
				County	
Nancy, daughter of Delia	19	Made free in East Florida 1816		House servant to Adam Cooper in Camden County	1821
John, son of Delia	17	Made free in East Florida 1816		Apprentice to house carpentry trade in St. Mary's	1821
Hetty, daughter of Delia	15	Made free in East Florida 1816		House servant to Adam Cooper in Camden County	1821
Keziah, daughter of Delia	13	Made free in East Florida 1816		House servant to Adam Cooper in Camden County	1821
Esther, daughter of Delia	11	Made free in East Florida 1816	Resides with Adam Cooper in Camden County		1821
Mary, daughter of Delia	9	Made free in East Florida 1816	Resides with Adam Cooper in Camden County		1821
Josiah, son of Delia	7	Made free in East Florida	Resides with Adam Cooper in		1821

Name	Age	Nativity	When Came to Georgia	Occupation	Date
		1816	Camden County		
Patty Tims	62	Made free by Mr. Tims	Resides Camden County since freedom 14 years ago.	Common laborer	1821
Cato Norris	68	Made free by will of Thomas Norris	Resides in St. Mary's, ever since his freedom	Carpenter	1822
Member Norris	57	Brought by Thomas Norris from Jamaica 32 years ago.	Sold to Charles Jackson, Esq. who emancipated her. Resides in St. Mary's ever since	Wash woman	1822
Balinda	68	Made free by will of Thomas Norris	Resides in St. Mary's ever since her freedom	Common Laborer	1822
Fanny Smith	33	Born in Georgia. Made free by will of John Aggerett 1813.	Resided principal part of her life in St. Mary's.	Shopkeeper	1822
George, son of Fanny	8	Born free in St. Mary's	Resides with his mother.	Mulatto	1822
Rosaline, daughter of Fanny	6	Born free in St. Mary's	Resides with his mother.	Mulatto	1822
Mary	42	Made free by will of	Formerly resided in	Common laborer.	1822

Name	Age	Nativity	When Came to Georgia	Occupation	Date
		John Tompkins in South Carolina.	East Florida, now St. Mary's	Mulatto	
Sipio, son of Mary	22	Born free in St. Mary's	Resides in St. Mary's	Carpenter	1822
Charles, son of Mary	21	Born free in St. Mary's	Resides in St. Mary's	Common laborer	1822
Henry, son of Mary	15	Born free in St. Mary's	Resides in St. Mary's with his mother		1822
Polly, daughter of Mary	13	Born free in St. Mary's	Resides in St. Mary's with her mother		1822
Willson, son of Mary	10	Born free in St. Mary's	Resides in St. Mary's with his mother		1822
Norris, son of Mary	6	Born free in St. Mary's	Resides in St. Mary's with his mother		1822
Amey, daughter of Mary	4	Born free in St. Mary's	Resides in St. Mary's with her mother		1822
William, son of Mary	8	Born free in St. Mary's	Resides in St. Mary's with his mother		1822
John, son of Mary	18 mos	Born free in St. Mary's	Resides in St. Mary's with his		1822

Name	Age	Nativity	When Came to Georgia	Occupation	Date
			mother		
Thomas Nepton	22	Born free in Georgia	Resides in St. Mary's	Sailor	1822
Charles Clark	21	Born free East Florida	Resides in St. Mary's	Laborer. Mulatto	1822
Reme Brunett	33	Born free, formerly resided Charleston, South Carolina	Resides in St. Mary's, 12 years	Merchant. Mulatto	1822
Clement Labattny	33	Born Santo Domingo	Resides in St. Mary's, 27 years	Mariner. Mulatto	1822
Suzett Duvall	38	Born free Santo Domingo	Resides in St. Mary's, 18 years	No occupation. Insane. Mulatto	1822
James Alfred Garjan	19	Born free. Formerly resided Charleston, South Carolina	Resides in St. Mary's, 11 years	Shopkeeper for Reme Brunett	1822
John Sipio	34	Born free. Formerly resided New Orleans	Resides in St. Mary's	Boatman. Mulatto	1822
Jacob Mure	54	Born Georgia	Resided principal part of his life in Camden County	Laborer	1822
Mariah		Africa	Purchased her freedom	House servant to	1822

Name	Age	Nativity	When Came to Georgia	Occupation	Date
			from George J. F. Clark in East Florida 1796. Formerly resided Augusta. Resides in St. Mary's since 1817.	George J. F. Clark	
Flora	43	Born Johns Island, South Carolina. Purchased her freedom from firm Panton Laslie & Co. East Florida 1796.	Resided in St. Mary's since 1817.	House servant o George J. F. Clark	1822
Pattey Tims	63	Made free by her master Mr. Tims, deceased.	Resided in Camden County 15 years, since freedom.	Common laborer	1822
Cato Norris	61	Made free by will of Thomas Norris	Resides in St. Mary's since his freedom	Carpenter	1823
Member Norris, wife of Cato	58	Came with owner Thomas Norris from Jamaica 33 years ago	Sold to Charles Jackson, Esq. who emancipated her. Resides in St. Mary's since coming	Wash woman	1823

Name	Age	Nativity	When Came to Georgia	Occupation	Date
			here.		
Reme Brunett	34	Born free. Formerly resided Charleston, South Carolina	Resides in St. Mary's, 13 years	Merchant. Mulatto	1823
James Alfred Gaujan	20	Born free. Formerly resided Charleston, South Carolina.	Resides St. Mary's, 12 years	Shopkeeper for Reme Brunett. Mulatto	1823
Mary Baird	43	Made free by will of John Thompkins in South Carolina	Formerly resided East Florida, now in St. Mary's	Common laborer. Mulatto	1823
Sipio, son of Mary	23	Born free in St. Mary's	Resides in St. Mary's	House carpenter. Mulatto	1823
Charles, son of Mary	22	Born free in St. Mary's	Resides in St. Mary's	Common laborer. Mulatto	1823
Henry, son of Mary	16	Born free in St. Mary's	Resides in St. Mary's with his mother	Common laborer. Mulatto	1823
Polly, daughter of Mary	14	Born free in St. Mary's	Resides in St. Mary's with her mother	Mulatto	1823
Willson, son of Mary	11	Born free in St. Mary's	Resides in St. Mary's with his	Mulatto	1823

44

Name	Age	Nativity	When Came to Georgia	Occupation	Date
			mother		
Norris, son of Mary	7	Born free in St. Mary's	Resides in St. Mary's with his mother	Mulatto	1823
Amey, daughter of Mary	5	Born free in St. Mary's	Resides in St. Mary's with her mother	Mulatto	1823
William, son of Mary	9	Born free in St. Mary's	Resides in St. Mary's with his mother	Mulatto	1823
John, son of Mary	2	Born free in St. Mary's	Resides in St. Mary's with his mother	Mulatto	1823
Patty Tims	64	Made free by master Mr. Tims about 16 years ago	Resides in Camden County	Common laborer	1823
Mariah		Africa. Purchased her freedom from George J. F. Clark East Florida 1796.	Formerly resided Augusta. Resides St. Mary's since 1817.	House servant o George J. F. Clark.	1823
Flora	44	Born Johns Island, South Carolina.	Purchased freedom from firm Panton Laslie & Co. East Florida 1796.	House servant to George J. F. Clark	1823

Name	Age	Nativity	When Came to Georgia	Occupation	Date
			Resides St. Mary's since 1817.		
Cato Norris	62	Made free by will of Thomas Norris	Resides in St. Mary's ever since freed	Carpenter	1824
Member Norris, wife of Cato	59	With owner Thomas Norris came from Jamaica 34 years ago.	Sold to Charles Jackson, Esq. who emancipated her. Resides in St. Mary's ever since her arrival in this country.	Wash woman	1824
Remie Brunett	35	Born free. Formerly resided Charleston, South Carolina.	Resides St. Mary's 14 years.	Merchant. Mulatto	1824
James Alfred Gaujan	21	Born free in Charleston, South Carolina.	Resides in St. Mary's 13 years.	Shopkeeper for R. Brunett	1824
Fanney Smith	35	Born Georgia. Made free by John Arggerett, deceased in East Florida 1813.	Resided principal part of her life in St. Mary's.	Shopkeeper	1824
George Arggerett, son of Fanney	10	Born free in St. Mary's.	Resides in St. Mary's with his	Mulatto	1824

Name	Age	Nativity	When Came to Georgia	Occupation	Date
			mother		
Rosaline Arggerett, daughter of Fanney	8	Born free in St. Mary's.	Resides in St. Mary's with her mother	Mulatto	1824
George Clarke	25	Born free in East Florida	Resides in St. Mary's since 1817	Tailor. Mulatto	1824
Mary Baird	44	Made free by will of John Thompkins in South Carolina.	Formerly resided East Florida. Now resides St. Mary's	Common laborer. Mulatto	1824
Scipio, son of Mary	24	Born free in St. Mary's	Resides in St. Mary's	House carpenter. Mulatto	1824
Charles, son of Mary	23	Born free in St. Mary's	Resides in St. Mary's	Common laborer. Mulatto	1824
Henry, son of Mary	17	Born free in St. Mary's	Resides in St. Mary's with his mother	Common laborer. Mulatto	1824
Polly, daughter of Mary	15	Born free in St. Mary's	Resides in St. Mary's with her mother	Common laborer. Mulatto	1824
Willson, son of Mary	12	Born free in St. Mary's	Resides in St. Mary's with his mother	Mulatto	1824
William, son of Mary	10	Born free in St. Mary's	Resides in St. Mary's with his	Mulatto	1824

Name	Age	Nativity	When Came to Georgia	Occupation	Date
			mother		
Norris, son of Mary	8	Born free in St. Mary's	Resides in St. Mary's with his mother	Mulatto	1824
Amey, daughter of Mary	6	Born free in St. Mary's	Resides in St. Mary's with her mother	Mulatto	1824
John, son of Mary	3	Born free in St. Mary's	Resides in St. Mary's with his mother	Mulatto	1824
Thomas Brister	24	Born free in Georgia	Resides in St. Mary's	Sailor	1824
Jack Ross	50	Born free	Resides in St. Mary's	Sailor	1824
James Baird, son of Mary Baird	1	Born free in St. Mary's	Resides in St. Mary's with his mother	Mulatto	1824
Patty Tims	65	Maid free by late master Mr. Tims	Resides in Camden County, 17 years	Common laborer	1824
Robert Hull	37	Born Wilmington, North Carolina	Made free by owner Ambrose Hull in East Florida 1821. Resides in Camden County with Miss Rebecca	Common laborer	1825

Name	Age	Nativity	When Came to Georgia	Occupation	Date
			Lewis.		
Remie Brunett	36	Born free Charleston, South Carolina	Resides St. Mary's 15 years	Merchant. Mulatto	1825
James Alfred Ganjan	22	Born free Charleston, South Carolina	Resides St. Mary's 14 years	Shopkeeper for R. Brunett, Mulatto	1825
Patty Tims	66	Made free by master Mr. Tims.	Resides Camden County 18 years since her freedom.	Common laborer	1825
Robert Hull	38	Born Wilmington, North Carolina.	Emancipated by Ambrose Hull in East Hull 1821. Now resides with Miss Rebecca Lewis	Common laborer	1826
Patty Tims	67	Made free by master Mr. Tims 19 years ago.	Resided in Camden County since freedom	Common laborer	1826
Rime Brunett	37	Born free and formerly resided Charleston, South Carolina.	Resides in St. Mary's 16 years.	Merchant. Mulatto	1826
James Alfred Gaujan	23	Born free Charleston, South	Resides in St. Mary's 15 years	Shopkeeper for R. Brunett.	1826

Name	Age	Nativity	When Came to Georgia	Occupation	Date
		Carolina.		Mulatto	
Robert Hull	39	Born Wilmington, North Carolina	Made free by Ambrose Hull in East Florida 1821. Resides in Camden County	Common laborer	1827
Patty Tims	68	Made free by master Mr. Tims 20 years ago	Resides in Camden County since freedom	Common laborer	1827
Reme Brunett	38	Born free Charleston, South Carolina.	Resides in St. Mary's 17 years.	Merchant & planter. Mulatto	1827
Robert Hull	40	Born Wilmington, North Carolina	Made free by Ambrose Hull in East Florida 1821. Resides in Camden County	Common laborer	1828
Patty Tims	69	Made free by master Mr. Tims 21 years ago	Resides in Camden County since freedom	Common laborer	1828
Reme Brunett	39	Born free Charleston, South Carolina.	Resides in St. Mary's 18 years.	Merchant & planter. Mulatto	1828
Bob Hull	42	Born Wilmington, North	Made free by Ambrose Hull in East Florida	Common laborer	1830

Name	Age	Nativity	When Came to Georgia	Occupation	Date
		Carolina	1821. Resides in Camden County		
Romeo	38	Born Charleston, South Carolina.	Made free by will of Alexander Grigon Charleston, South Carolina 1809. Resides Camden County 3 years.	Carpenter. Mulatto	16 Apr 1831
Charles	30	Born free in St. Mary's.	Resided all his life in St. Mary's	Common laborer. Mulatto	5 May 1831
Harry	32	Made free in East Florida by Silvester Silva 1823.		Ship carpenter. Mulatto	5 May 1831
Filla	27	Made free in East Florida by Sylvester Silva 1829.		House keeper	5 May 1831
Joanna, daughter of Filla	8	Made free in East Florida in 1829			5 May 1831
Elizabeth Brewer	30	Born free in East Florida	Resides in St. Mary's	Seamstress	
Georgia Ann, daughter of	6	Born free in			

Name	Age	Nativity	When Came to Georgia	Occupation	Date
Elizabeth		St. Mary's			
Alonzo, son of Elizabeth	5	Born free in St. Mary's			
Edwin, son of Elizabeth	3	Born free in St. Mary's			
Eliza Brewer	19	Born free in East Florida	Resides in St. Mary's	Seamstress. Mulatto	
Sipio Baird	30	Born free in St. Mary's	Resides in St. Mary's	House carpenter. Mulatto	
Henry Baird	24	Born free in St. Mary's	Resides in St. Mary's	House carpenter. Mulatto	
Thomas Mure		Born free in Georgia	Resided principal part of his life in Georgia, now in St. Mary's	House carpenter. Mulatto	
Cato Norris	80	Made free by will of Thomas Norris	Resides in St. Mary's since freedom	House carpenter	
Bob Hull	43	Born Wilmington, North Carolina	Made free by Ambrose Hull in East Florida 1821. Resides in Camden County	Common laborer	
Patty Tims	71	Made free by her master Mr.	Resides in Camden County since	Common laborer	

52

Name	Age	Nativity	When Came to Georgia	Occupation	Date
		Tims	emancipation		
Bob Hull	44	Born Wilmington, North Carolina	Made free by Ambrose Hull in East Florida 1821	Common laborer	1832
Patty Tims	72	Made free by her master Mr. Tims 24 years ago	Resides in Jefferson, Camden County since emancipation	Common laborer	1832
Romeo	39	Born Charleston, South Carolina	Made free by will of Alexander Grigor at Charleston 1809. Resides in Camden County.	Carpenter. Mulatto	1832
Bob Hull	45	Born Wilmington, North Carolina	Made free by Ambrose Hull in East Florida 1821	Common laborer	1833
Patty Tims	73	Made free by her master Mr. Tims 25 years ago	Resides in Jefferson, Camden County since emancipation	Common laborer	1833
Romeo	40	Born Charleston, South Carolina	Made free by will of Alexander Grigor at Charleston 1809. Resides in Camden County.	Carpenter. Mulatto	1833

Name	Age	Nativity	When Came to Georgia	Occupation	Date
Bob Hull	45	Born Washington, North Carolina	Made free by Ambrose Hull in East Florida 1821	Common laborer	1834
Patty Tims	74	Made free by her master 26 years ago	Resides in Jefferson, Camden County since emancipation	Common laborer	1834
Romeo	41	Born Charleston, South Carolina	Made free by will of Alexander Grigor at Charleston 1809. Resides in Camden County.	Carpenter. Mulatto	1834
Harry King	35	Made free by Silvester Silva in East Florida 1823		Ship carpenter. Mulatto	1832, 1833, 1834 (See register in this book of his name Harry for 5 May 1831.)
Matilda	31	Made free by Silvester Silva in Florida 1829.		Yellow	(This register is for 1832, 1833, 1834.)
Elizabeth Brewer	33	Born free in East Florida	Resides in St. Mary's	Seamstress. Mulatto	Registered for 1832, 1833, 1834

Name	Age	Nativity	When Came to Georgia	Occupation	Date
Eliza Brewer	21	Born free in East Florida	Resides in St. Mary's	Mulatto	Registered for 1832, 1833, 1834
Georgia Ann Brewer, daughter of Elizabeth	9	Born free in St. Mary's		Mulatto	Registered for 1832, 1833, 1834
Alonzo Brewer, son of Elizabeth	8	Born free in St. Mary's		Mulatto	Registered for 1832, 1833, 1834
Edward Brewer, son of Elizabeth	6	Born free in St. Mary's		Mulatto	Registered for 1832, 1833, 1834
Julia Ann Brewer, daughter of Elizabeth	2	Born free in St. Mary's		Mulatto	Registered for 1832, 1833, 1834
Sipio Baird	33	Born free in St. Mary's	Resides in Camden County	House Carpenter. Mulatto	Registered for 1832, 1833, 1834
Charles Baird	36	Born free in St. Mary's	Resides in Camden County	Mulatto	Registered for 1832, 1833, 1834
Joseph Emanuel		Born free in Portugal	Resides in Georgia upwards of 20 years, now in St. Mary's	Painter	Registered for 1832, 1833, 1834
Romeo	42	Born Charleston,	Made free by will of	Carpenter.	17 Sep

Name	Age	Nativity	When Came to Georgia	Occupation	Date
		South Carolina	Alexander Grigor at Charleston 1809. Resides in Camden County.	Mulatto	1839
Bob Hull	52	Born Washington, North Carolina.	Made free by Ambrose Hull in East Florida 1821. Resides Camden County.	Common laborer	1 Jul 1840
Romeo	47	Born Charleston, South Carolina	Made free by will of Alexander Gregorie 1809. Resides in Camden County	Carpenter. Mulatto	1 Jul 1840
Bob Hull	53	Born Washington, North Carolina.	Made free by Ambrose Hull in East Florida 1821. Resides Camden County.	Common laborer	5 Jul 1841
Romeo	48	Born Charleston, South Carolina	Made free by will of Alexander Gregorie 1809. Resides in Camden County	Carpenter. Mulatto	5 Jul 1841

Name	Age	Nativity	When Came to Georgia	Occupation	Date
John Pearce	19	Born free in Savannah	Working with G. W. Curns 4 years in Habersham County and in Salilla. Resides in Camden County.	Carpenter	28 Mar 1842
Bob Hull	53	Born Washington, North Carolina.	Made free by Ambrose Hull in East Florida 1821. Resides Camden County.	Common laborer	1842
Romeo	48	Born Charleston, South Carolina	Made free by will of Alexander Gregorie 1809. Resides in Camden County	Carpenter. Mulatto	1842
William Middleton	23	Born free in Fernandina	Resides in St. Mary's	Carpenter. Mulatto	
Emanuel	53	Born free. Formerly resided in Portugal Lisbon	Resides in St. Mary's 32 years	Mariner. Mulatto	
Thomas Delany	26	Born free in St. Mary's	Raised in St. Mary's	Carpenter. Mulatto	1843
Allen	22	Born free in Camden	Resides in Camden	Laborer	20 May 1842

Name	Age	Nativity	When Came to Georgia	Occupation	Date
		County	County		
Tom Brister	47	Born free in Providence, Nassau County	Lived in Camden County 36 years.	Farmer	1844
Romeo	50	Born Charleston, South Carolina	Made free by will of Alexander Gregorie 1809. Resides in Camden County	Carpenter. Mulatto	1844
William Middleton	24	Born free in Fernandina	Resides in St. Mary's	Carpenter. Mulatto	1844
Emanuel	54	Born free. Formerly resided in Portugal Lisbon	Resides in St. Mary's 33 years	Mariner. Mulatto	1844
Thomas Delany	27	Born free in St. Mary's	Raised in St. Mary's	Carpenter. Mulatto	1844

Clarke County

In 1958, the Genealogical Society of Salt Lake City, Utah microfilmed the original record book held by the Superior Court in the courthouse at Athens, Georgia. A copy is available in the microfilm reading room of the Georgia Department of Archives and History in Morrow, Georgia. The heading on the microfilm roll reads

Inferior Court
Clarke County
State of Georgia
Mixed Records
County Officers Bonds, Free Persons Book
No Index 1842-1872

Diagonally across the first page, the clerk wrote

Clark County Inferior Court
Free Persons of Color, 1847-1862
County Officers Bonds for year 1864 (First 8 pages)

In back of book (Inferior and Superior Court)
Petitions for Limited Partnership – 1842 – 53 – 72
And Charter for Trustees Synagogue of Israel – 1872.

The following transcription includes only the information concerning the free persons of color. The clerks entered the registrations in a variety of formats over the years, even recording different information; hence, the transcription repeats some records in their entirety and presents most registrations in a standardized tabular format.

State of North Carolina
Caswell County

I M. Abisha Slade Clerk of the Court of Pleas and Quarter Sessions for Caswell County hereby Certify that Green Bass a man of Colour now of the State of Georgia, but formerly of Caswell County, North Carolina, is a free man. And that at October Court of Pleas and Quarter Sessions held for he County of Caswell in 1827, the said Green Bass was bound as an Apprentice to one Abel Royster. I further Certify that the said Green Bass was universally known in the neighborhood where he was raised to be a free boy.

In Testimony whereof I have hereunto set my hand and affirmed my seal of Office this 18th day of September 1844. M. Slade, Clk of Caswell County Court

State of North Carolina
Caswell County

I John E. Brown Presiding Magistrate of the County Court of Caswell County Certify that Abisha Slade is Clerk of the County Court aforesaid, duly qualified as such, and as such that due faith and credit is due and of right ought to be paid to his Official Acts.

Given under my hand as Presiding Magistrate aforesaid this 18th day of September 1844. John E. Brown, P. M.   Recorded   20th   September 1844

Georgia   Inferior Court October Term 1847
Clarke County

Ordered that Jonas Lassiter be admitted to registration in terms of law, he having in Open Court upon the Oath of Thomas Stewart proven his freedom to the satisfaction of the Court after notice duly published in terms of the Statute.

Ordered that Grunel Bass be admitted to registry as a free Person of Colour having filed Satisfactory evidence with Clerk of his freedom, and notice of Application having been duly Published in terms of the Statute.

Georgia   Clerks Office Inferior Court
Clarke County

The above two orders extracted as far as concerned the act of Registry from the minutes of said Court.

Given under my hand at Office this 26th day of October 1847.   John Calvin Johnson, Clerk

Name	Age	Occupation	Residence	Height	Form	Color	Remarks
Greene Ross in Georgia 1835	32	Barber, Cook, Stallion Keeper	Athens	5-8	Chunky or Heavy	Almost White	Certificate 26 Oct 1847
Jonas Lassiter born in Georgia	21	Farmer	Wildfiel District	5-11	Light & Active	Very Bright Mulatto	Certificate 26 Oct 1847
Michael Smith in Georgia 1847	60	Farmer	Scull Shoal District	5-10½	Light & Active	Dark	Certificate 1 Feb 1848
Jane Miller born in Georgia							
Bernard Onendine in Georgia 1843	29	Farmer	221 District	5-8 or 9	Light & Active	Very Bright Mulatto	Certificate 24 Apr 1848
Robert Henderson in Georgia 30 years	55	Farmer	Buncombe District	5-10	Light & Active	Dark	Certificate 24 Apr 1848
Mary Lassiter born in Georgia							
Henderson Mitchell born in Virginia in Georgia 20 years	37	Groomer	Perigord's District	5-8½	Light & Active	Mulatto	Certificate 25 Apr 1848
Charles Chubb							

Name	Age	Occupation	Residence	Height	Form	Color	Remarks
Lewis A. Pettiford in Georgia 34 years	77	Farmer	Salem District	5-6½	Chunk Built	Mulatto	Certificate 22 May 1848
Antoinette Pettiford born in Georgia	30	Farmer Wife	Salem District	5-7	Light & Active	Mulatto	Certificate 22 May 1848
Jacob Man in Georgia 20 years	37	Farmer	Sandy Creek District	5-8	Light	Mulatto	Certificate 25 May 1848
Milley May in Georgia 20 years	38	Cook	Sandy Creek District	Tall	Light	Mulatto	Certificate 25 May 1848
Dolly Man in Georgia 20 years	54	Ordinary	Aaron Brigg's Sandy Creek District	Middle	Medium	Dark Yellow	Certificate 5 Jun 1848
Michael Smith	61						1 Feb 1849
Bryant Onendine	30						24 Apr 1849
Henderson Mitchell	38						25 Apr 1849, 1850, 1851, 1852, 1853, 1853, 1855, 1856, 1857, 1858
Jacob Man							25 May 1849, 1850,

Name	Age	Occupation	Residence	Height	Form	Color	Remarks
							1851, 1852, 1853, 1854, 1855
Bryant Onendine	31						24 Apr 1850
Robert Henderson	56	Farmer	Buncomb District	5-10	Bulk	Dark	24 Apr 1849
Robert Henderson	57	Farmer	Buncomb District	5-10	Bulk	Dark	24 Apr 1850
Robert Henderson	58	Farmer	Buncomb District	5-10	Bulk	Dark	24 Apr 1851
Robert Henderson	59	Farmer	Buncomb District	5-10	Bulk	Dark	24 Apr 1852
Robert Henderson	60	Farmer	Buncomb District	5-10	Bulk	Dark	24 Apr 1853
Robert Henderson	61	Farmer	Buncomb District	5-10	Bulk	Dark	24 Apr 1854
Robert Henderson	62	Farmer	Buncomb District	5-10	Bulk	Dark	24 Apr 1855
Robert Henderson	63	Farmer	Buncomb District	5-10	Bulk	Dark	24 Apr 1856

Georgia   } Called Inf^r Court for Special Purposes 1st Feby 1848
Clarke County

Ordered that Michael Smith a free person of Color be admitted to register as a free person of Color in terms of the Statue he having filed his papers with the Clerk and proven his freedom by Lindsey Durham, Junior and that Lindsey Durham is appointed his Guardian in terms of the law and of he annexed assent.

Wm Pickens, J. I. C.
H. F. Nunnally, J. I. C.
J. W. Barrett, J. I. C.

A true Extract from minutes 1st Feby 1848

Names	Age	Occupation	Residence	Height	Form	Color	Date
Milledge Mann	21	Blacksmith	Clarke County	Medium	Medium	Dark	20 Oct 1854
Jacob Mann	17	farmer	Clarke County	Medium	Medium	Black	20 Oct 1854
Dolly Mann	15	Field Hand	Clarke County	Medium	Medium	Almost Mulatto	20 Oct 1854
James Mann	18	Harness Maker	Athens	Medium	Medium	Mulatto	8 May 1855
Hannah Pettiford	20	House Woman	Near Salem	Medium	Medium	Mulatto	12 Mar 1856
John Pettiford	19	Farmer	Near High Shoals	Medium	Medium	Mulatto	12 Mar 1856
William Pettiford	17	Farmer	Near Salem	Medium	Medium	Mulatto	12 Mar 1856
Elder Pettiford	16	Farmer	Near Salem	Medium	Medium	Mulatto	12 Mar 1856
William Man	21	Farmer & Shoemaker	Jno. Nance's	6-0	Heavy Built	Dark	18 Sep 1851 1 Jul 1852 1 Jul 1853 1 Jul 1854 1 Jul 1855

Names	Age	Occupation	Residence	Height	Form	Color	Date
							1 Jul 1856 1 Jul 1857 1 Jul 1858 1 Jul 1859 1 Jul 1860 1 Jul 1861 1 Jul 1862
Lewis A. Pettiford	77						22 May 1849
Lewis A. Pettiford	78						22 May 1850
Lewis A. Pettiford	79						22 May 1851
Lewis A. Pettiford	80						22 May 1852
Lewis A. Pettiford	81						22 May 1853
Lewis A. Pettiford	82						22 May 1854
Lewis A. Pettiford	83						22 May 1855
Lewis A.	84						22 May

Names	Age	Occupation	Residence	Height	Form	Color	Date
Pettiford							1856
Ann Man	21	Washer	Athens	5-6	Slender	Very Light	14 Mar 1853

Emanuel County

The Genealogical Society of Salt Lake City, Utah microfilmed the original record book held by the Inferior Court in the courthouse at Swainsboro, Georgia. A copy is available in the microfilm reading room of the Georgia Department of Archives and History in Morrow, Georgia. On the first page, the clerk wrote

A Book for Registering the names of free persons of Color
By Ezekiel Clifton, Clerk of the Superior and Inferior Court of Emanuel County
July the 16th 1855

The clerk entered the registrations in narrative form, each entry a short paragraph. The first entry reads in full

Matthew Kirkland, Free person of Color, aged 28 years, Resident of Burke County, Occupation Farming, Complexion Yellow, With some inclination to Freckle, Height 5 feet 10 or 11 Inches, this 10th July 1853. E. Clifton, Clk.

The following transcription extracts the relevant information from the original record and presents it in a standardized tabular format.

Name	Age	Residence	Occupation	Description	Date
Matthew Kirkland	28	Burke County	Farming	Complexion yellow, with some inclination to freckle. 5-10 or 11.	10 Jul 1853
Burt Kirkland	25 or 30	Burke County	Farming	Complexion Yellow. 5-10	10 Jul 1853
James Williams	52			Yellow complexion. 5-10. Farmer	5 Jul 1853
Jiney Clark, wife of James	41			Yellow complexion. 5-0. Seamstress	5 Jul 1853
Elbert Clark, son of Jiney	21			Yellow complexion. 5-10. Farmer	5 Jul 1853
Henry Clark, son of Jiney	18			Yellow complexion. 5-4. Farmer	5 Jul 1853
Dorcas Clark, daughter of Jiney	15			Yellow complexion. Seamstress	5 Jul 1853
Charles Wigg	66	Emanuel County	Farmer	Yellow complexion. 5-10. John C. Luise, Gurdian	5 Jul 1854
Polly Wigg, wife of Charles	35			Seamstress. John C. Luise, Guardian	5 Jul 1854
James Williams	52	Emanuel County	Farmer	Yellow complexion. 5-10.	5 Jun 1854

Name	Age	Residence	Occupation	Description	Date
Jincy Clark, wife of James	41	Emanuel County	Seamstress	Yellow complexion. 5-0	5 Jun 1854
Elbert Clark, son of Jincy	21	Emanuel County	Farmer	Yellow complexion. 5-11	5 Jun 1854
Henry Clark, son of Jincy	18	Emanuel County	Farmer	Yellow Complexion. 5-4.	5 Jun 1854
Dorcas Clark, daughter of Jincy	15	Emanuel County	Seamstress	Yellow complexion	5 Jun 1854
Counail McCuller	18 or 19	Emanuel County	Farming	Yellow Complexion. 5-11, Benjamin Shuron, Agent.	5 Jul 1854
Sarah Angeline Rose, daughter of Nancy Rose	15	Emanuel County	Farming	Yellow Complexion. 5-0.	5 Jul 1854
Roxyann Richardson, daughter of Elizabeth Richardson	19	Emanuel County	Farming	Yellow complexion	5 Jul 1854
Carley Wigg	66	Born South Carolina	Farming	Yellow complexion. 5-10. Alexander Brinson, Guardian	4 Jul 1855
Polly Swan	35		Seamstress	Yellow complexion. 5-2. Alexander Brinson, Guardian	4 Jul 1855

Name	Age	Residence	Occupation	Description	Date
William Swan	16		Farmer	Yellow complexion. 5-4. Alexander Brinson, Guardian	4 Jul 1855
Edward Thomas Swan	14		Farmer	Yellow complexion. 5-0. Alexander Brinson, Guardian.	4 Jul 1855
James Williams	52		Farming	Yellow complexion. 5-10.	4 Jul 1855
Jincy Clark, wife of James	41		Seamstress	Yellow complexion. 5-6.	4 Jul 1855
Elbert Clark, son of Jincy	21		Farming	Yellow complexion. 510.	4 Jul 1855
Henry Clark, son of Jincy	18		Farming	Yellow complexion. 5-4.	4 Jul 1855
Dorcas Clark, daughter of Jincy	15		Seamstress	Yellow complexion. 5-4.	4 Jul 1855
Sarah Angeline Rose	16		Seamstress	Yellow complexion. 5-0. Aashley Pritchard, Guardian	4 Jul 1855
Damaris Rose	16 or 18		Farming or seamstress	5-0. Aashley Pritchard, Guardian	4 Jul 1855
Burt Kirkland	27		Farming	High yellow complexion. 5-10, Irvin	4 Jul 1855

Name	Age	Residence	Occupation	Description	Date
				Kirkland, Guardian	
Matthew Kirkland	28		Farming	Yellow complexion. 5-10 or 11. Irvin Kirkland, Guardian	4 Jul 1855
Council McCuller	19		Farming	Yellow complexion. 5-11.	4 Jul 1855
James Williams	55		Farming	Yellow complexion. 5-10.	8 May 1856
Jincy Clark, wife of James	45		Seamstress	Yellow complexion. 5-6.	8 May 1856
Elbert Clark, son of James Williams & Jincy Clark				Yellow complexion. 5-10.	8 May 1856
Henry Clark, son of Jincy	21		Farming	Yellow complexion. 5-10.	8 May 1856
Dorcas Clark, daughter of Jincy	18		Seamstress	Yellow complexion. 5-5.	8 May 1856
James Williams	15		Farming	Yellow complexion. 5-[blot].	8 May 1856
James Clark			Farming	Yellow complexion. 5-6.	8 May 1856
Sarah Kelly	40		Seamstress	Yellow complexion.	8 May 1856

Name	Age	Residence	Occupation	Description	Date
Miles Cilley	19	Born in Burke County	Farming	Yellow complexion. 6-2.	
Frances Kelly	17	Born in Burke County	Farming	Yellow complexion. 5-0.	
Charles Wig	65		Farming	Yellow complexion. 5-8. 150 pounds.	7 Jul 1856
Polly Wig, wife of Charles	45		Common house business		7 Jul 1856
William [blot], son of Charles Wig	18			5-8	7 Jul 1856
Raley Richardson	19	Born in Emanuel County	Common house business	Yellow complexion. 5-6. 135 pounds. Ashley E. Wiggens	7 Jul 1856
Sarah Angeline Rose	19 or 20	Born in Emanuel County. Resides in Bibb County, near Macon.	House business & farming	Yellow complexion. 5-0. William A. Pritchard, Guardian	7 Jul 1856
Demaris Rose	17 or 18	Born in Emanuel County	House & working on farm	Yellow complexion. 5-6. William A. Pritchard, Guardian	7 Jul 1856
Mathew Kirkland	29		Farming	Yellow complexion. 5-10 or 11. Irvin Kirkland,	7 Jul 1856

Name	Age	Residence	Occupation	Description	Date
				Guardian	
Burt Kirkland	28		Farming	Yellow complexion. 5-10. Irvin Kirkland, Guardian	7 Jul 1856
Councel McCullough	20		Farming	Yellow complexion. 5-11. John P. Sherrard	4 Aug 1856
Charles Wig	66		Farming	Yellow complexion. 5-8. Alexander C. Brinson, Guardian	28 Jun 1857
Polly, wife of Charles	46		Common house business	5-0. Alexander C. Brinson, Guardian	28 Jun 1857
William Swan, son of Charles Wig	19		Farming	5-8. Alexander C. Brinson, Guardian	28 Jun 1857
Demaris Rose			Common field hand	5-6. 140 pounds. Yellow complexion.	1 Jul 1857
James Clark	45		Farming	Yellow complexion. 5-7.	1 Jul 1857
Sarah Clark, wife of James	44		House business.	Dark complexion. 5-7. 120 pounds.	1 Jul 1857
Miles Clark, son of James & wife	20		Farming	5-11. 140 pounds.	1 Jul 1857
Frances Clark, son	17		Farming	5-7. 130	1 Jul

Name	Age	Residence	Occupation	Description	Date
of James & wife				pounds.	1857
Perciliann Clark, daughter of James & wife	14		Seamstress	5-0. 125 pounds	1 Jul 1857
James Williams	57		Farmer	Yellow complexion. 5-9. 226 pounds	1 Jul 1857
Dorcas, daughter of James Williams	20		Household business	5-0. 125 pounds	1 Jul 1857
James, son of James Williams	13		Farmer	Yellow complexion. 5-0. 130 pounds	1 Jul 1857
Elbert Clark, son of James	23		Farming	Yellow complexion. 5-9. 146 pounds	1 Jul 1857
Henry Clark	22		Farming	Yellow complexion. 5-10 or 11. John P. Sherrard	
Mathew Kirkland	30		Farming	Yellow complexion. 5-10 or 11. 170 or 175 pounds. John P. Sherrard	
John Clark	30 or 35		Farming	Yellow complexion. 165 or 170 pounds. John P. Sherrard	
Julia Clark, wife of				John P.	

Name	Age	Residence	Occupation	Description	Date
John				Sherrard	
Council McCullough	22		Farming	Yellow complexion. 5-11 or 12. 150 pounds. John P. Sherrard	6 Jul 1857
Rockann Richardson, daughter of Elizabeth Richardson	20		Farming	Yellow complexion. 5-5.	6 Jul 1857
Mathew Kirkland	31		Farming	Yellow complexion. 5-10 or 11. 170 or 175 pounds. John P. Sherrard, Guardian	6 Feb 1858
Julia Clark, wife of Mathew Kirkland			House business	5-5. John P. Sherrard, Guardian	6 Feb 1858
James Williams	58		Farming	5-10. 226 pounds.	6 Feb 1858
Dorcas Williams, daughter of James	21		Household business	5-5. 130 pounds.	6 Feb 1858
James Williams, son of James	14		Farming	5-6. 130 pounds	6 Feb 1858
Sally Kelly	42		Seamstress	Dark complexion. 5-3. 120 or 25 pounds	6 Feb 1858

Name	Age	Residence	Occupation	Description	Date
Frank Kelly, son of Sally	18		Farming	Dark complexion. 5-7.	6 Feb 1858
Priscilia Ann Kelly, daughter of Sally	15		Household business	Mulatto complexion. 5-2. 125 pounds	6 Feb 1858
Henry Williams, formerly known as Henry Clark	25		Farming	Yellow complexion. 5-10 or 11. 150 or 60 pounds.	22 Mar 1858
Charles Wig	67		Farming	Yellow complexion. 5-8. 150 pounds. Alexander C. Brinson, Guardian	
Polly Wig, wife of Charles	46		Common house business	Yellow complexion. Alexander C. Brinson, Guardian	
Edward Swan, son of Charles & Polly Wig	14		Farming	Yellow complexion. 5-8 or 10. 140 pounds. Alexander C. Brinson, Guardian	
James Clark	46		Farming	Yellow complexion. 5-7. 161 pounds. John Oglesby, Guardian	12 Jun 1858

Name	Age	Residence	Occupation	Description	Date
Elbert Williams, son of James Williams	24		Farming	Yellow complexion. 5-9. 160 pounds	1 Jul 1858
Roxann Richardson, daughter of Elizabeth Richardson	21	Born in Emanuel County		Yellow complexion. 5-8. 145 pounds	1 Jul 1858
James William, Sr.	59	Born in Barnwell District, South Carolina	Farming	Yellow complexion. 5-10 or 11. 230 pounds	2 Apr 1859
James Williams, Jr., son of James, Sr.	22	Born in Burke County	Farming	Yellow complexion. 5-10. 160 pounds	2 Apr 1859
Dorcas Williams, daughter of James, Sr.	22	Born in Burke County	Common house business	Yellow complexion. 5-0. 130 pounds	2 Apr 1859
Charles Wig	68		Farming	Yellow complexion. 5-8. 150 pounds. Alexander C. Brinson, Guardian	6 Jun 1859
Polly Wig, wife of Charles	47		House business	Yellow complexion. 5-0. 130 or 40 pounds. Alexander C. Brinson, Guardian	6 Jun 1859
Edward Swan, son	17	Resides in Richmond	Draying	Yellow complexion.	6 Jun

Name	Age	Residence	Occupation	Description	Date
of Charles Wig		County		160 pounds. Alexander C. Brinson, Guardian	1859
John Clark	31		Farming	Yellow complexion. 165 or 170 pounds	25 Jul 1859
Mathew Kirkland	32		Farming	Yellow complexion. 5-10 or 11. 170 pounds	25 Jun 1859
Julia Clark					
Francis Kelly	19		Farming	5-7 or 8. 140 or 50 pounds	25 Jun 1859
James Clark	46		Farming	5-9. 161 pounds	25 Jun 1859
Sarah Kelly	45		Seamstress	Dark complexion. 5-7. 120 pounds	25 Jun 1859
Priscillia Ann Kelly	16		Seamstress	Yellow complexion. 5-2. 125 pounds.	25 Jun 1859
Henry Williams	24		Farming	5-10 or 11. 150 or 60 pounds	25 Jun 1859
Elbert Williams	25		Farming	Yellow complexion. 5-9. 155 pounds	25 Jun 1859
Roxey Ann	22	Born in	Farming	Yellow	24

Name	Age	Residence	Occupation	Description	Date
Richardson		Emanuel County		complexion. 5-8. 140 pounds	Jun 1859
Henry Williams	25		Farming	Yellow complexion. 5-10 or 11. 160 pounds	25 Apr 1860
Elbert Clark	26		Farming	Yellow complexion. 5-10 or 11. 155 pounds	28 Jun 1860
John Clark	32		Farmer	Yellow complexion. 170 pounds	28 Jun 1860
Priscilla Ann Kelly	17		Seamstress	Yellow complexion. 5-2.	28 Jun 1860
Frances Carter	18		Seamstress	Yellow complexion. 5-8	28 Jun 1860
James Williams, Sr.	60	Born in Barnwell District, South Carolina	Farming	Yellow complexion. 5-10 or 11. 230 pounds	28 Jun 1860
James Williams, Jr.	23	Born in Burke County	Farming	5-10. 150 pounds	28 Jun 1860
Eliza Williams	36			Yellow complexion. 4-2.	28 Jun 1860
James Clark	47		Farming	5-9. 161 pounds	28 Jun 1860
Francis Kelly	20		Farming	5-7 or 8. 140	28

Name	Age	Residence	Occupation	Description	Date
				or 50 pounds	Jun 1860
Sarah Kelly	46		Seamstress	Dark complexion. 5-7. 120 pounds	28 Jun 1860
Mathew Kirkland	33	Born in Burke County	Farming	Yellow complexion. 5-10 or 11. 170 pounds	28 Jun 1860
Julia Clark	30			Yellow complexion. 120 pounds	28 Jun 1860
Roxey Ann Ritckerson	23	Born in Emanuel County	Farming & common house business	Yellow complexion. 5-8. 140 pounds	29 Jun 1860
Thomas Williams	16	Born in Emanuel County	Farming	Yellow complexion. 5-0.	2 Jul 1860
Charles Wig	69		Farming	Yellow complexion. 5-8. 150 pounds. Alexander C. Brinson, Guardian	2 Jul 1860
Polly Wig	48		House business	Yellow complexion. 5-0. 230 pounds. Alexander C. Brinson, Guardian	2 Jul 1860
Edward Swan	18			Yellow complexion. 160 pounds.	2 Jul 1860

Name	Age	Residence	Occupation	Description	Date
				Alexander C. Brinson, Guardian	
Dorcas Swan	23	Born in Burke County	Common house business	Yellow complexion. 5-0. 180 pounds. Alexander C. Brinson, Guardian	2 Jul 1860
James Clark	50			5-9. 161 pounds. John Oglesby, Guardian	25 May 1861
Sarah Kelly, wife of James Clark	47		Family & sewing	5-7. 120 pounds. John Oglesby, Guardian	25 May 1861
Henry ~~Clark~~ Williams	25		Farming	5-8. 180 pounds, John P. Sherrod, Guardian	25 May 1861
John Clark	33		Farming	5-10. 170 pounds. John P. Sherrod, Guardian	25 May 1861
Rocksey Ann Richerson	24	Born in Emanuel County	Farming & common house business	Yellow complexion. 5-8. 140 pounds	21 Jun 1861
Matthew Kirkland	34	Born in Burke County	Farming	Yellow complexion. 5-10 or 11. 170 pounds	29 Jun 1861
Julia Clark, wife of Matthew Kirkland	31			Yellow complexion.	29 Jun

Name	Age	Residence	Occupation	Description	Date
				120 pounds	1861
Charles Wig	70		Farming	Yellow complexion. 5-8. 150 pounds. Alexander C. Brinson, Guardian	1 Jul 1861
Polly Wig	60		House business	Yellow complexion. 5-0. 230 or 40 pounds. Alexander C. Brinson, Guardian	1 Jul 1861
Edward Swan	19			Yellow complexion. 160 pounds. Alexander C. Brinson, Guardian	1 Jul 1861
Darcas Swan	24	Born in Burke County	Common house business	Yellow complexion. 5-0. 130 pounds. Alexander C. Brinson, Guardian	1 Jul 1861
James Williams, Sr.	61	Born in Barnwell District, South Carolina	Farming	Yellow complexion. 5-10 or 11. 230 pounds	1 Jul 1861
Thomas Williams, son of James, Sr.	15			Yellow complexion. 5-11. 151 pounds	1 Jul 1861

Name	Age	Residence	Occupation	Description	Date
Matilda Williams, daughter of James, Sr.	14			Yellow complexion. 4-5. 121 pounds	1 Jul 1861
James Williams, Jr., son of James, Sr.	24	Born in Burke County		5-10. 150 pounds	1 Jul 1861
Eliza Williams	37		Farming	High yellow complexion. 4-2.	1 Jul 1861
Elbert Clark	27		Farming	Yellow complexion. 5-10 or 11. 155 pounds	1 Jul 1861
Frances Carter, wife of Elbert Clark	19		Seamstress	Yellow Complexion. 5-8.	1 Jul 1861
Francis Kelley	21		Farming	5-7 or 8. 140 or 50 pounds. John Oglesby, Guardian.	1 Jul 1861
James Williams, Sr.	62	Born in Barnwell District, South Carolina	Farming	Yellow complexion. 5-10 or 11. 185 pounds. William Sherrod, Guardian	7 Apr 1862
Thomas Williams, son of James, Sr.	16		farming	Yellow complexion. 5-10. 150 pounds. William Sherrod, Guardian	7 Apr 1862
Matilda Williams, daughter of James,	15			Yellow complexion. 4-5. 120	7 Apr

Name	Age	Residence	Occupation	Description	Date
Sr.				pounds. William Sherrod, Guardian	1862
James Williams, Jr., son of James, Sr.	25	Born in Burke County		5-10. 150 pounds. William Sherrod, Guardian	7 Apr 1862
Eliza Williams, wife of James, Jr.	38		Farming	High yellow complexion. 4-2. William Sherrod, Guardian	7 Apr 1862
Henry Williams	27		Farming	Yellow complexion. 5-10 or 11. 150 or 160 pounds.	11 May 1862
James Clark	51			5-9. 161 pounds. John Oglesby, Guardian	23 Jun 1862
Sarah Kelly, wife of James Clark	48		Farming & sewing	5-7. 120 pounds. John Oglesby, Guardian	23 Jun 1862
Francis Kelly	22		Farming	5-7 or 8. 140 or 50 pounds	22 Jun 1862
Josephine Kelly, wife of Francis	17		Spinning	Yellow complexion. 4-8 or 10.	22 Jun 1862
Charles Wig	60		Farming	140 pounds	6 Jun 1862

Name	Age	Residence	Occupation	Description	Date
Polly Wig, wife of Charles	50		Housekeeping & farming		6 Jun 1862
Edward Swann	20		Farming	Yellow complexion. 160 pounds.	6 Jun 1862
Darcas Swann, wife of Edward	25		Common house business	Yellow complexion. 5-0. 130 pounds	6 Jun 1862
James Williams, Jr.	25	Born in Burke County		5-10. 150 pounds	6 Jun 1862
Roxey Ann Richerson	24	Born in Emanuel County	Common house business	Yellow complexion. 140 pounds	26 Jun 1862
Sarah Clark					
Matthew Kirkland	34	Born in Burke County	Farming	Yellow complexion. 5-10 or 11. 170 pounds	3 Jul 1862
Julian Kirkland	31			Yellow complexion. 120 pounds	3 July 1862
Henry Williams	28		Farming	Yellow complexion. 5-10 or 11. 150 pounds.	14 Feb 1863
Hambleton Dukes	20		Farming	Light complexion. 5-8.	2 Mar 1863
James Williams	23		Farming	Yellow complexion. 5-8 or 9. 175 pounds.	10 Apr 1863

Name	Age	Residence	Occupation	Description	Date
Frances Kelly	25		Farming	Light complexion. 5-6. 160 pounds	10 Apr 1863
Edward Swan	21		Farming	Yellow complexion. 5-6 or 8. 160 pounds. A. C. Brinson, Guardian	18 Apr 1863
Darcas Swan	26		Common house business	Yellow complexion. 5-0. 130 pounds. A. C. Brinson, Guardian	18 Apr 1863
Josephine, wife of Frank Kelly	16		Common house business	Yellow complexion. 5-0. 125 pounds	29 Apr 1863
James Clark	52		Farming	5-9. 150 pounds	
Sarah Kelly, wife of James Clark	49	Born in Emanuel County	Farming	5-7. 120 pounds	
Raymond Clark					
Missouri, wife of Raymond Clark					
Elbert Clark	29	Born in Burke County	Farming	Yellow complexion. 5-10. 160 pounds	17 Jun 1863
Francis Clark, wife of Elbert	21		Seamstress	Yellow complexion. 5-8.	17 Jun 1863

Name	Age	Residence	Occupation	Description	Date
Thomas Williams	17	Born in Emanuel County	Farming	Yellow complexion. 5-10 or 11. 165 pounds. William Sherrod, Guardian	17 Jun 1863
Matilda Williams	16	Born in Emanuel County	Farming	Yellow complexion. 4-5. 140 pounds. William Sherrod, Guardian	17 Jun 1863
Eliza Williams	39	Born in Chatham County	Farming	High yellow complexion. 4-2. William Sherrod, Guardian	17 Jun 1863
Charles Wig	72		Farming	Yellow complexion. 5-8. 150 pounds. A. C. Brinson, Guardian	17 Jun 1863
Polly Wig, wife of Charles	62		House business	Yellow complexion. 235 pounds. A. C. Brinson, Guardian	17 Jun 1863
Matthew Kirkland	35	Born in Burke County	Farmer	Yellow complexion. 170 pounds	29 Jun 1863
Julia Kirkland, wife of Matthew	32			Yellow complexion. 125 pounds	29 Jun 1863
John Clark	41	Born in	Farming	Yellow complexion.	1 Jul

Name	Age	Residence	Occupation	Description	Date
		Burke County		170 pounds. John P. Sherrod, Guardian	1863
Selia Ann Clark, wife of John	18		House business	Yellow complexion. 130 pounds. John P. Sherrod, Guardian	1 Jul 1863
Sarah Clark	30	Born in Burke County		Yellow complexion. 125 pounds	1 Jul 1863
Ned Kelly	23	Born in Emanuel County	Farming	Dark complexion. 5-6, `150 pounds. J. W. Oglesby, Agent	19 Jul 1863
Council C. McCuller	25	Born in Emanuel County	Carpenter	High yellow complexion. 6-1. 160 pounds. Benj. Sherrod, Agent	4 Apr 1864
Raymond Clark	47	Born in Burke County	Carpenter	Yellow complexion. 5-10 or 11. 145 pounds	2 May 1864
Jas. Clark	57	Born in Burke County	Farming	High yellow complexion. 5-6. 150 pounds	16 May 1864
Sarah Clark, wife of Jas.					16 May 1864
Henry Williams	29	Born in Burke County	Miller & farmer	Yellow complexion.	16 May

Name	Age	Residence	Occupation	Description	Date
				5-6.	1864
Polly Williams, wife of Henry	18				16 May 1864
John Clark	39			5-9. 160 pounds	16 May 1864
Celia Clark, wife of John	17		Cook & washer in Co. K, 28th Geo.	Yellow complexion.	16 May 1864
Francis Kelly	26	Born in Burke County	Farming	Yellow complexion. 5-6. 160 pounds	16 May 1864
Josephine, wife of Francis Kelly					16 May 1864
Elbert Clark	31	Born in Burke County	Farming & blacksmith	Yellow complexion.	16 May 1864
Frances, wife of Elbert Clark	20				16 May 1864
Elizuse Williams, wife of Jas. Williams	40		Farming	High yellow complexion. 4-2. Wm Sherrod, Guardian	25 May 1864
Tilda Williams	17	Born in Burke County	Farming	Yellow complexion. 4-5. 120 pounds. Wm Sherrod, Guardian	25 May 1864
James Williams	23		Farmer	Yellow	25

Name	Age	Residence	Occupation	Description	Date
				complexion. 5-8 or 9. 150 pounds. Dan[1] B. Johnson, Guardian	May 1864
Matthew Kirkland	36	Born in Burke County	Farmer	Yellow complexion. 170 pounds	2 Jun 1864
Julia Kirkland, wife of Matthew	32			Yellow complexion. 125 pounds	2 Jun 1864
Edward Kelly	26		Farmer	Black complexion. 5-6. 140 pounds. John Oglesby, Guardian	6 Jun 1864
Rocksey Ann Richardson	26	Born in Emanuel County	Farmer & common house work	Yellow complexion. 140 pounds	20 Jun 1864
Hamp Dukes	24	Born in Burke County	Farming	Yellow complexion. 5-6. 150 pounds. D. B. Johnson, Guardian	Jun 1864
Elbert Clark	22	Born in Burke County	Farmer	Dark complexion. 6-0. A. C. Brinson, Guardian	Jun 1864
Darkas, wife of Elbert Clark	25			Dark yellow complexion. A. C. Brinson, Guardian	Jun 1864
Charles Wig	70			Yellow complexion.	Jun

Name	Age	Residence	Occupation	Description	Date
				5-8. A. C. Brinson, Guardian	1864
Wife of Charles Wig	50			Very dark complexion. A. C. Brinson, Guardian	Jun 1864
Thomas Williams	18			Yellow complexion. 5-10. 130 pounds	Jun 1864
Sarah Clark	35		House work	Yellow complexion	Jun 1864

Jones County

In 1966, the Genealogical Society of Salt Lake City, Utah microfilmed the original record book held by the Superior Court in the courthouse at Gray, Georgia. A copy is available in the microfilm reading room of the Georgia Department of Archives and History in Morrow, Georgia. The heading on the microfilm roll reads

Jones County
Georgia
Court of Ordinary
Inferior Court Minutes
Writs
1818-1846

On the first page, the clerk wrote

Samuel Jones & Philes Jones & Nat Jones, Jerry Jones P 1

On the second page, the clerk wrote

Nathaniel Mathews
Lear Mathews
Nancy Mathews
Hamblin Ooslem

Jonathan Parker

The actual registrations begin on the next page, the clerk entering each registration in a short paragraph. The following is a full transcription of the first page.

April 1818. Clerks Office

Came in to office Samuel Jones and inroled himself as a man of coller. Is a native of Georgia, by profession a Farmer, age twenty one years.

Philes Jones a woman of coller came In to office and inroled her name, as by profession a spiner, age sevinteen years old.

Nat Jones a boy of coller came in to office and inroled his name, by profession a farmer, a Native of Georgia, age sixteen years old.

Jerry Jones a boy of coller came into office, age nine months old. Native of Georgia

The following table presents the relevant information from the registry in a standard format.

Name	Age	Nativity	In Georgia How Long	Occupation	Date
Samuel Jones	21	Georgia		Farmer	Apr 1818
Philes Jones	17			Spinner	
Nat Jones	16	Georgia		Farmer	
Jerry Jones	9 mos	Georgia			
Nathaniel Mathews	58	Virginia	In Jones County, Georgia 31 years	Farmer	
Lear Mathews	50	North Carolina	35 years	Spinner	
Nancy Mathews	12	Georgia		Spinner	
Hamlin Ooslam	10	Georgia			
Jenny	37	Virginia	25 years	House business. John Humphries, Guardian	8 Apr
Solomon	21	Georgia	21 years	Blacksmith. John Humphries, Guardian	
Woodliff	18	Georgia	18 years	Farmer. John Humphries, Guardian	
Berry	4	Georgia	4 years	John Humphries, Guardian	
Stephen	2	Georgia	2 years	John Humphries, Guardian	

Name	Age	Nativity	In Georgia How Long	Occupation	Date
Warren Williams	34	North Carolina	17 years	Farmer	9 Apr
Howell Furguson	25	Virginia	12 years	Turner	11 Apr
Jacob Edmunds	47	Virginia	12 years	Farmer	3 May
Jerry Dandridge	23	New Kent County, Virginia	22 years	Farmer	
Ceaser	62	Barter County, North Carolina	4 years	Farmer	3 Feb 1820
Nero	60	North Carolina	35 years	Farmer	
Sarah Mills	25	Mecklenburg County, North Carolina	1 year	Seamstress	7 Feb 1820
Jenny	38	Virginia	26 years	House business. John Humphries, Guardian	
Solomon	21	Georgia	21 years	Blacksmith. John Humphries, Guardian	
Berry	5	Georgia	5 years	John Humphries, Guardian	
Stephen	2	Georgia	2 years	John Humphries, Guardian	

Name	Age	Nativity	In Georgia How Long	Occupation	Date
Nathaniel Mathews	63	Virginia	34 years	Farmer	23 Feb 1820
Lear Mathews	51	North Carolina	36 years	Spinner	23 Feb 1820
Nancy Mathews	13	Georgia	13 years	Spinner	23 Feb 1820
Tom Cousins	27	North Carolina	19 years	Farmer	29 Feb 1820
Pat Cousins	48	Virginia	17 years	Spinner	29 Feb 1820
James Cousins	39	North Carolina	17 years	Blacksmith	29 Feb 1820
Doly Cousins	31	North Carolina	17 years	Spinner	29 Feb 1820
Russell Cousins	8	Georgia	8 years		29 Feb 1820
Martha Cousins	6	Georgia	6 years		29 Feb 1820
Caroline Cousins	4	Georgia	4 years		29 Feb 1820
Mary Cousins	2	Georgia	2 years		29 Feb 1820

Name	Age	Nativity	In Georgia How Long	Occupation	Date
Milley	16	North Carolina	4 years	House business. John Pitman, Guardian	
West	13	North Carolina	4 years	Farmer. John Pitman, Guardian	
Fany Jones	40	North Carolina	3 weeks	Spinner. James Daniel, Guardian	6 Mar 1820
Harry Jones	12	North Carolina	3 weeks	Farmer. James Daniel, Guardian	6 Mar 1820
Charles Jones	10	North Carolina	3 weeks	Plowboy. James Daniel, Guardian	6 Mar 1820
Giney Jones	3	North Carolina	3 weeks	James Daniel, Guardian	6 Mar 1820
Milley Jones	8 mos	North Carolina	3 weeks	James Daniel, Guardian	6 Mar 1820
Mariah Jones	14	Georgia	3 weeks	Spinner. Egbert P. Daniel, Guardian	
Jeferson Jones	7	Georgia	3 weeks	Egbert P. Daniel, Guardian	
Peter Jones	5		3 weeks	Egbert P. Daniel	
Samuel Jones	22	Georgia		Farmer. Frederick Daniel,	

Name	Age	Nativity	In Georgia How Long	Occupation	Date
				Guardian	
Philis Jones	18	Georgia		Spinner. Frederick Daniel, Guardian	
Nat Jones	17	Georgia		Farmer. Frederick Daniel, Guardian	
Je[blot] Jones	18 mos	Georgia		Frederick Daniel, Guardian	
Howell Ferguison	25		13 years	William W. Brown, Guardian	
Jacob Edmunds	48	Virginia	3 years	Farmer	7 Apr 1820
Dandridge	24	Virginia	22 years	Farmer	
Hamlin Ooslam	11	Georgia		Plowboy	
Warren Williams	36	North Carolina	19 years	Farmer	Feb 1821
Nathaniel Mathews	60	Virginia	40 years	Farmer	6 Mar 1821
Lear Mathews	52	North Carolina	37 years	Spinner	6 Mar 1821
Nancy Mathews	14	Jones County		Spinner	6 Mar 1821
Hamlin Oslan	12	Jones		Plowboy	6 Mar

Name	Age	Nativity	In Georgia How Long	Occupation	Date
		County			1821
Howell Ferguison	26	Virginia	14 years	Farmer	10 Mar 1821
Thomas Cousins	28	North Carolina	20 years	Farmer	17 Mar 1821
James Cousins	40		18 years	Blacksmith	17 Mar 1821
Jacob Edmuns	48	Virginia	5 years	Farmer	4 May 1821
Milly Braswell	15	North Carolina	5 years	Spinster. John Vance, Guardian	28 May 1821
David Epps	21	North Carolina		Farmer. John Vance, Guardian	28 May 1821
Fanny Jones	40	North Carolina	18 years	Spinster. James Daniel, Guardian	28 May 1821
Harry Jones	13	Georgia	1 year	Farmer. James Daniel, Guardian	28 May 1821
Charles Jones	11	Georgia	1 year	Plowboy. James Daniel, Guardian	28 May 1821
Milley Jones	20 mos	Georgia	1 year	James Daniel, Guardian	28 May 1821
Ginny Jones	4	Georgia	1 year	James Daniel, Guardian	28 May

Name	Age	Nativity	In Georgia How Long	Occupation	Date
					1821
Mariah Jones	15	Georgia	1 year	Spinster. Egbert P. Daniel, Guardian	28 May 1821
Jefferson Jones	8	Georgia	1 year	Egbert P. Daniel, Guardian	28 May 1821
Peter Jones	6	Georgia	1 year	Egbert P. Daniel, Guardian	28 May 1821
Nat Jones	18	Georgia	18 years	Farmer. Frederick Daniel, Guardian	28 May 1821
Phillis Jones	19	Georgia	19 years	Spinster. Frederick Daniel, Guardian	28 May 1821
Jerry Jones	2	Georgia	2 years	Frederick Daniel, Guardian	28 May 1821
Ginny	38	Virginia	26 years	Spinster. John Humphries, Guardian	28 May 1821
Solomon	22	Georgia	22 years	Waiter. John Humphries, Guardian	28 May 1821
Berry	6	Georgia	6 years	John Humphries, Guardian	28 May 1821
Stephen	4	Georgia	4 years	John Humphries, Guardian	28 May 1821

Name	Age	Nativity	In Georgia How Long	Occupation	Date
Caroline	6 mos	Georgia		John Humphries, Guardian	28 May 1821
Howell Ferguson	27	Virginia	15 years, Resides Houston County	Turner	3 Apr 1822
Jinny	40	Virginia	27 years	Spinster. John Humphries, Guardian	28 May 1821
Thomas	23	Georgia		Waiter. John Humphries, Guardian	28 May 1821
Berry	7	Georgia		John Humphries, Guardian	28 May 1821
Stephen	5	Georgia		John Humphries, Guardian	28 May 1821
Caroline	18 mos	Georgia		John Humphries, Guardian	28 May 1821
Nathaniel Mathews	56	North Carolina	34 years	Farmer	9 Jul 1822
Leah, wife of Nathaniel	50	North Carolina	35 years	Spinner	9 Jul 1822
Nancy Mathews, daughter of Nathaniel	15	Georgia		Spinner	9 Jul 1822
Tarlton Francis Smothers	23	Georgia		Farmer. William W. Brown, Guardian	

Name	Age	Nativity	In Georgia How Long	Occupation	Date
Sally Cousins	35	North Carolina	20 years	Spinster. Charles L. Cannon, Guardian	11 Jun 1823
Russell	12	Georgia		Charles L. Cannon, Guardian	11 Jun 1823
Martha	10	Georgia		Charles L. Cannon, Guardian	11 Jun 1823
Caroline	8	Georgia		Charles L. Cannon, Guardian	11 Jun 1823
Mary	6	Georgia		Charles L. Cannon, Guardian	11 Jun 1823
John	4	Georgia		Charles L. Cannon, Guardian	11 Jun 1823
Arnold	2	Georgia		Charles L. Cannon, Guardian	11 Jun 1823
Fany Jones	42	North Carolina	20 years	Spinster. James Daniel, Guardian	20 Jun 1823
Henry Jones	15	Georgia		Farmer. James Daniel, Guardian	20 Jun 1823
Charles Jones	13	Georgia		Plowboy. James Daniel, Guardian	20 Jun 1823
Jinny Jones	6	Georgia		James Daniel, Guardian	20 Jun 1823

Name	Age	Nativity	In Georgia How Long	Occupation	Date
Milly Jones	4	Georgia		James Daniel, Guardian	20 Jun 1823
Jacob Edmonds	51	Virginia	7 years	Farmer	8 Jul 1823
Nathaniel Mathews	57	North Carolina	35 years	Farmer	8 Jul 1823
Leah, wife of Nathaniel Mathews	51	North Carolina	36 years	Spinner	8 Jul 1823
Nancy, daughter of Nathaniel Mathews	16	Georgia		Spinner	8 Jul 1823
Sawney	30	North Carolina	5 years	Farmer	4 Aug 1823
Stephen Herrod	25	Georgia		Laborer. David T. Milling, Guardian	20 Oct 1823
Jenny Jones	43	North Carolina	21 years	Spinster. James Daniel, Guardian	16 Feb 1824
Harry Jones	16	Georgia		Farmer. Blackman, James Daniel, Guardian	16 Feb 1824
Ch^s Jones	14	Georgia		Plowboy. James Daniel, Guardian	16 Feb 1824
Jinny Jones	7	Georgia		James Daniel, Guardian	16 Feb 1824
Milly Jones	5	Georgia		James Daniel, Guardian	16 Feb

Name	Age	Nativity	In Georgia How Long	Occupation	Date
					1824
William King					16 Feb 1824
Jerry Jones	6	Georgia		William Dismukes, Guardian	27 Feb 1824
Jacob Edmunds		Virginia			20 Nov 1824
Fanny Jones	44	North Carolina	22 years	Spinster. James Daniel, Guardian	11 Jul 1825
Harry Jones	17	Georgia		Farmer. James Daniel, Guardian	11 Jul 1825
Jones	15	Georgia		Blacksmith. James Daniel, Guardian	11 Jul 1825
Jenny Jones	8	Georgia		James Daniel, Guardian	11 Jul 1825
Milly Jones	6	Georgia		James Daniel, Guardian	11 Jul 1825
Jacob Edmunds	55	Virginia		Farmer	25 Jul 1825
Fanny Jones	45	North Carolina	23 years	Spinster. James Daniel, Guardian	17 Mar 1826
Harry Jones	18	Georgia		Farmer. James Daniel,	17 Mar

Name	Age	Nativity	In Georgia How Long	Occupation	Date
				Guardian	1826
Charles Jones	15	Georgia		Farmer. James Daniel, Guardian	17 Mar 1826
Jenny Jones	9	Georgia		Spinster. James Daniel, Guardian	17 Mar 1826
Milly Jones	7	Georgia		Spinster. James Daniel, Guardian	17 Mar 1826
Nathaniel Mathews	67	North Carolina	37 years	Farmer	3 Apr 1826
Lear, wife of Nathaniel Mathews	53	North Carolina	38 years	Spinner	3 Apr 1826
Nancy, daughter of Nathaniel Mathews	18	Georgia		Spinner	3 Apr 1826
Handlin Ouslam	17	Georgia		Farmer	3 Apr 1826
Jacob Edmunds	63	Virginia	11 years	Farmer	20 Jul 1826
Suthey Perregine	21	North Carolina	9 months	Spinster	
Lucinda Pagens Ana	25	North Carolina		Spinster	
Jacob Edmunds	61				15 Mar 1831

Morgan County

The clerks entered the original registrations in a short paragraph format, each entry or group of entries signed by the clerk. The following table presents the relevant information from each registration in a standardized format, omitting the clerk's names.

Registry of the names of free Persons of Colour   T. L. King, Dep.

Name	Age	Nativity	When came to Georgia	Occupation	Date
Jeremiah Chavis		Born 14 Feb 1757 South Carolina	1769	Cooper	Apr 1819
Nancy Waters	24	South Carolina	Resided in Georgia 17 years	Spinner	Apr 1819
Robert Carrel	31	North Carolina	1816	Farmer	14 Apr 1819
Hannah Grant	59	North Carolina	Resided in Georgia 40	Spinner	Apr 1819
Anderson Grant	35	Georgia		Carpenter	Apr 1819
Daniel Stuart	50	Virginia	1790	Carpenter	Apr 1819
Billy Ferguson	60	Near Williamsburg, Virginia	1785	Farmer	3 May 1819
Green Roberts	25	North Carolina	About 25 years ago	Farmer	25 Feb 1820
Daniel Stewart	50	Mecklenburg County, North Carolina	1790	Carpenter	2 Mar 1820
Robert Carrel	32	North Carolina	1816	Farmer	2 Mar 1820

Name	Age	Nativity	When came to Georgia	Occupation	Date
Jeremiah Cheaves		Born 1757 South Carolina	1769	Cooper	2 Mar 1820
Hannah Grant	60	North Carolina	Resided in Georgia 41 years	Spinner	27 Jun 1820
Anderson Grant	36	Georgia		Carpenter	27 Jun 1820
Nancy Waters	25	South Carolina	1801	Spinner	27 Jun 1820
Liley Waters	21	South Carolina	1801	Spinner	27 Jun 1820
Robert Carrel	33	North Carolina	1816	Farmer	3 Apr 1821
Jeremiah Chevas		Born 1757 South Carolina	1769	Cooper	18 Jun 1821
Daniel Stewart	51	Virginia	1790	Carpenter	4 Jun 1821
Jeremiah Chevas		Born 1757 North Carolina	1769	Cooper	1 May 1822
Robert Carrel	34	North Carolina	1816	Farmer	3 Jun 1822
Ned Dempsey		Born 1802 North Carolina	1821	Farmer	3 Aug 1824 also 22 Aug 1824

Name	Age	Nativity	When came to Georgia	Occupation	Date
James Shrarley	24	Virginia	Last of Jan 1827. Now resides at Lewis Maguire's	Farmer	12 Mar 1828
John Bird	32	Halifax County, North Carolina	1821. Now resides in Madison	barber	2 July 1829
Eliza Bird	17	Elbert County		Spinner	2 Jul 1829
John Bird	33	Halifax County, Virginia	1821	Barber	27 Feb 1830
Eliza Bird	17	Elbert County		Spinner	27 Feb 1830
Margaret Ann Bird, daughter of John and Eliza Bird		Born 7 Apr 1828 Macon, Bibb County			27 Feb 1830
Martha Ann Bird		Born 20 Dec 1829 Milledgeville			27 Feb 1830
Robert Friend		Born 1814 Guilford County, North Carolina	Feb 1832	Blacksmith	1 Mar 1832
Polly Chub	18	Rockingham County, North Carolina	Feb last	Weaver, spinner, &c	1 Mar 1832
Nancy, daughter of Polly Chub	16 mos				1 Mar 18321
John Bird	34	Halifax County, North	1821. Now resides in	Barber	7 Mar 1834

Name	Age	Nativity	When came to Georgia	Occupation	Date
		Carolina	Madison.		
Eliza Bird, wife of John Bird	18	Petersburgh, Georgia		Spinner	7 Mar 1834
Margaret A. Bird, daughter of John and Eliza Bird	6	Macon, Bibb County			7 Mar 1834
Martha A. Bird, daughter of John and Eliza Bird	2	Milledgeville			7 Mar 1834
Laura Antoinette Bird, daughter of John and Eliza Bird		Born 1 Nov 1833			7 Mar 1834
Isaac Chubb	43	Rockingham County, North Carolina	7 Jan 1830	Blacksmith. Miller H. Harny, Guardian	24 Nov 1838
Mary Chubb	28	Rockingham County, North Carolina		Spinster. Miller H. Harny, Guardian	24 Nov 1838
William Chubb, son of Isaac & Nancy Chubb	11			Farmer. Miller H. Harny, Guardian	24 Nov 1838
Nancy Chubb, daughter of Isaac & Nancy Chubb	7			Farmer. Miller H. Harny, Guardian	24 Nov 1838
Henry Chubb, son of Isaac & Nancy Chubb	5	Morgan County		Miller H. Harny, Guardian	24 Nov 1838
Amma Chubb, daughter of Isaac	3	Morgan County		Miller H. Harny,	24 Nov

Name	Age	Nativity	When came to Georgia	Occupation	Date
& Nancy Chubb				Guardian	1838
John Chubb, son of Isaac & Nancy Chubb	10 mos	Morgan County		Miller H. Harny, Guardian	24 Nov 1838
Judy Kelley	48			Baker. Black complexion. L. Groves, Guardian	15 Feb 1841
James Kelly, son of Judy Kelly	13			No calling. L. Groves, Guardian	15 Feb 1841
Emily Kelly, daughter of Judy Kelly	23			Washer & seamstress. L. Groves, Guardian	15 Feb 1841
Lowder Kelly, child of Judy Kelly	16			Washer & seamstress. L. Groves, Guardian	15 Feb 1841
John Anderson	42	Greene County		Shoemaker. Black complexion.	15 Jun 1842
Daniel	60 or 65	Virginia		Washer. Dark complexion.	6 Aug 1842
Isaac Chubb	42	Rockingham County, North Carolina	7 Jan 1830	Blacksmith	15 Feb 1839
Mary, wife of Isaac Chubb	5	Rockingham County, North Carolina		Spinster	15 Feb 1839
William, child of Isaac Chubb		North Carolina			15 Feb 1839

Name	Age	Nativity	When came to Georgia	Occupation	Date
Nancy, child of Isaac Chubb		North Carolina			15 Feb 1839
Henry, child of Isaac Chubb	10				15 Feb 1839
Amanda, child of Isaac Chubb	9				15 Feb 1839
John, child of Isaac Chubb	3				15 Feb 1839
Isaac Chubb	43	Rockingham County, North Carolina	7 Jan 1830	Blacksmith. Miltin H. Hainey, Guardian	4 Dec 1841
Mary, wife of Isaac Chubb	35	Rockingham County, North Carolina		Spinster. Miltin H. Hainey, Guardian	4 Dec 1841
William, child of Isaac Chubb	11	North Carolina	Famer	Miltin H. Hainey, Guardian	4 Dec 1841
Nancy, child of Isaac Chubb	10	North Carolina	Famer	Miltin H. Hainey, Guardian	4 Dec 1841
Henry, child of Isaac Chubb	10	Morgan County		Miltin H. Hainey, Guardian	4 Dec 1841
Amanda, child of Isaac Chubb	9	Morgan County		Miltin H. Hainey, Guardian	4 Dec 1841
John, child of Isaac Chubb	3	Morgan County		Miltin H. Hainey,	4 Dec 1841

Name	Age	Nativity	When came to Georgia	Occupation	Date
				Guardian	
Archey Sorwin	35 or 40	Rockingham County, North Carolina	10 years ago	Farmer. Yellow complexion. Miltin H. Hainey, Guardian	6 Dec 1841
Madison Benefield	31			Blacksmith. Dark complexion. Wilks Graves, Guardian	15 Feb 1841
Judy Ruff	30			Washer. Black complexion. Wilks Graves, Guardian	15 Feb 1841
Victoria	2 mos	North Carolina		Wilks Graves, Guardian	15 Feb 1841
William Summerfield	13	North Carolina		Barber. Brown complexion. ~~Milton H. Hainey~~, Guardian. Approved 6 Dec 1841. Gone.	28 Jul 1842.
Rebecah Hawkins	26	Born 1815 Greene County. Resides Madison.		Seamstress, washer & baker. Josiah E. Matto, Guardian	6 Aug 1841
Elijah, son of Rebecah Hawkins	6	Madison		Josiah E. Matto, Guardian	6 Aug 1841

Name	Age	Nativity	When came to Georgia	Occupation	Date
Lewis, son of Rebecah Hawkins	3	Madison		Josiah E. Matto, Guardian	6 Aug 1841
Victoria	2	Madison		Josiah E. Matto, Guardian	6 Aug 1841
Daniel Stewart		MacKlingburg County, Virginia	1790	Carpenter. James C. Blont, Guardian	6 Dec 1841
Madison Benefield	32	North Carolina		Blacksmith. Dark complexion	24 Feb 1843
Judy Ruff	31	North Carolina		Washer. Black complexion	24 Feb 1843
Victoria	14 mos				24 Feb 1843
Rebecah Hawkins	26	Born 1815 Greene County		Seamstress, washer & baker	24 Feb 1843
Elijah, son of Rebecah Hawkins	6	Born Madison			24 Feb 1843
Lewis, son of Rebecah Hawkins	4	Born Madison			24 Feb 1843
Victoria, daughter of Rebecah Hawkins	2	Born Madison			
Isaac Chubb & family					5 Jun 1843

Name	Age	Nativity	When came to Georgia	Occupation	Date
Berliza Humphries	31	Born 1812 Green County		Seamstress, washer & baker	22 Feb 1848
Elijah Humphries, her son	31	Madison County			22 Feb 1848
John Humphries, her son	3	Madison County			22 Feb 1848
Isaac Chubb & family					4 Mar 1842
Edward Brooks	35	Born 1812 Chesterfield County, Virginia	1833	Osler & trainer. Mulatto. Height 5-5. Lewis Graves, Guardian	15 Jul 1847
Edward Brooks	36	Born 1812 Chesterfield County, Virginia	1833	Osler & trainer. Mulatto. Height 5-5. Lewis Graves, Guardian	15 Jul 1848
~~Edward Brooks~~		~~Born 1812 Chesterfield County, Virginia~~	~~1833~~	~~Osler & farmer. Mulatto. Height 5-5.~~ L. Graves, Guardian	15 Jul 1849
Rebecah Hawkins	32	Born 1815 Greene County. Resides Madison		Seamstress, washer & baker.	14 Feb 1849
Elijah, son of Rebecah Hawkins	14	Madison			14 Feb 1849

Name	Age	Nativity	When came to Georgia	Occupation	Date
John, son of Rebecah Hawkins	4	Madison			14 Feb 1849
Phenix, child of Rebecah Hawkins	7 mos	Madison			14 Feb 1849
Isaac Chub	48	Rockingham County, North Carolina	7 Jan 1830		14 Feb 1849
Mary Chubb	40	Rockingham County, North Carolina		Spinster	14 Feb 1849
William Chubb	18			Farmer. 4 feet high	14 Feb 1849
Nancy Chubb	17			Farmer. 4 feet 3	14 Feb 1849
Henry Chubb	13			Famer. 5 feet high	14 Feb 1849
Amanda Chubb	11			Farmer. 4 feet 2.	14 Feb 1849
John Chubb	10			Famer. 3 feet 10.	14 Feb 1849
James Benefield	19	Richmond County		Blacksmith. Dark complexion. 5 feet 7.	19 Jun 1849
Isaac Chub	50	Rockingham County, North Carolina	7 Jan 1830	Blacksmith. Yellow complexion.	19 Jun 1849

Name	Age	Nativity	When came to Georgia	Occupation	Date
				M. H. Hainey, Guardian	
Mary Chubb	48	Rockingham County, North Carolina		Spinster. Yellow complexion. 5 feet high. M. H. Hainey, Guardian	
William Chubb	19	Morgan County		Farmer. Yellow complexion. 5 feet 6.	19 Jun 1849
Nancy Chubb	17	Morgan County		Spinster. 5 feet high	19 Jun 1849
Amand Chubb	12	Morgan County		Spinster. Mulatto. 4 feet high	19 Jun 1849
John Chubb	11	Morgan County		Farmer. 5 feet 10	19 Jun 1849
Daniel Scott	28	Born 1822 Brunswick County	1829	Blacksmith. Yellow complexion. 6 feet high. Woodley Scott, Putnam County, Guardian. W. V. Burny acts for him.	8 Jan 1851
Edward Brook		Born 1812 Chesterfield County, Virginia	1833	Ostler, farmer & well digger. Mulatto. 5-8¾ high. L. Graus,	20 Jun 1851

Name	Age	Nativity	When came to Georgia	Occupation	Date
				Guardian	
Isaac Chub	52	Rockingham County, North Carolina	7 Jan 1830	Blacksmith. Yellow complexion. 5-10 high. Milton Hainey, Guardian	29 Jun 1851
Mary Chubb, wife of Isaac Chubb	48	Rockingham County, North Carolina	7 Jan 1830	Spinster & farmer. Yellow complexion. 5-2 high. Milton Hainey, Guardian	29 Jun 1851
William Chubb	21	Morgan County		Farmer. Yellow complexion. 5 feet 6. M. H. Hainey, Guardian	29 Jun 1851
Nancy Chubb, daughter of Isaac & Mary Chubb	19	Morgan County		Spinster. Mulatto. 5-10 high. M. H. Hainey, Guardian	29 Jun 1851
Henry Chubb, son of Isaac & Mary Chubb	16	Morgan County		Farmer. Yellow complexion. 5-2 high.	29 Jun 1851
Amanda Chubb, daughter of Isaac & Mary Chubb	14	Morgan County		Spinster & washer. Yellow complexion. 5-6 high.	29 Jun 1851
John Chubb, son of Isaac & Mary	10	Morgan County		Farmer. 5 feet 10	29 Jun

Name	Age	Nativity	When came to Georgia	Occupation	Date
Chubb					1851
Titus Gibbings	40	Georgia		Farmer. 5-3 high. James Griggs, of Putnam County, Guardian	25 Dec 1851
William Lasiter	33	Clarke County		Brick layer & plasterer. Yellow complexion. 5-10 high. Black hair. Black eyes	1 Jan 1852
Isaac Chub	53	Rockingham County, North Carolina	7 Jan 1830	Blacksmith. Yellow complexion. 5-10 high.	12 Jun 1853
Mary Chubb, wife of Isaac Chubb	45	Rockingham County, North Carolina	7 Jan 1830	Yellow complexion. 5-2 high.	12 Jun 1852
Nancy Chubb, daughter of Isaac & Mary Chubb	20	Morgan County		Spinster. Yellow complexion. 4-6 high. M. H. Hainey, Guardian	12 Jun 1852
Henry Chubb, son of Isaac & Mary Chubb	17	Morgan County		Farmer. Yellow complexion. 5-4 high.	12 Jun 1853
Amanda Chubb, daughter of Isaac & Mary Chubb	11	Morgan County		Spinster & washer. Yellow complexion. 4 feet high.	12 Jun 1852

Name	Age	Nativity	When came to Georgia	Occupation	Date
Isaac Chub	54	Rockingham County, North Carolina	7 Jan 1830	Blacksmith. Yellow complexion. 5-10 high.	16 Jun 1853

Pulaski County

In 1858, the Genealogical Society of Salt Lake City, Utah microfilmed the original record book held by the Inferior Court in the courthouse at Hawkinsville, Georgia. A copy is available in the microfilm reading room of the Georgia Department of Archives and History in Morrow, Georgia. The heading on the microfilm roll reads

Pulaski County
State of Georgia
Court of Ordinary
Minutes
1817-1865

A note inside the volume reads

Hartford Minutes, 1817-1865
Also
A Register of free negroes in Pulaski County, 1840-1865

The clerk entered each registration in a paragraph format. The first entry reads

A Register of the names of free persons of Collour

Oliff Thomas, a Woman about forty eight Years of age. Born in Sampson County, North Carolina, residing in Hawkinsville, Pulaski County, Georgia, time of coming Into his State unknown, occupation washing &c. Registered August 5th 1840. John V. Mitchell, Clk I. C.

The following table presents the relevant information extracted from the original record.

Name	Age	Place of Nativity	Residence	Time of Coming into Georgia	Occupation	Date
Oliff Thomas	48	Sampson County, North Carolina	Hawkinsville	Unknown	Washing &c	5 Aug 1840
Penny Padgett	38	Sampson County, North Carolina	Hawkinsville	Unknown	Washing &c	5 Aug 1840
Peggy Williams	43	Sampson County, North Carolina	Hawkinsville	1801	Washing &c	5 Aug 1840
Elizabeth Williams and her six children	39	Georgia	Hawkinsville		Washing &c	5 Aug 1840
Michael Williams, a girl	15	Georgia				5 Aug 1840
William Riley Williams	13	Georgia				5 Aug 1840
Elizabeth Matilda Williams	12	Georgia				5 Aug 1840
Joseph Williams	11	Georgia				5 Aug 1840
Lurancy Williams	5	Georgia				5 Aug 1840
Frank	6	Georgia				5 Aug

Name	Age	Place of Nativity	Residence	Time of Coming into Georgia	Occupation	Date
Williams	mos					1840
John Calvin Padgett, son of Penny Padgett	5	Jefferson County	Hawkinsville			5 Aug 1840
John Bird	39	Halifax County, North Carolina	Hawkinsville	1821	Barber	5 Aug 1840
Ephraim Newsome	31	Jefferson County	Pulaski County		Farming & boating	5 Aug 1840
Dread Newsome	29	Jefferson County	Pulaski County		Farmer & boater	
Loucinda Newsome, wife of Dred	22	Georgia	Pulaski County		Washing &c	
Moses, son of Dred and Loucinda Newsome	6	Georgia	Pulaski County		Washing &c	
Dread, son of Dred and Lucinda Newsome	3	Georgia	Pulaski County			
Margaret, daughter of Dread and Loucinda Newsome	2	Georgia	Pulaski County			
Jordan Scott	30	Martin County,	Hawkinsville	Unknown	Boatman	10 Aug

Name	Age	Place of Nativity	Residence	Time of Coming into Georgia	Occupation	Date
		North Carolina				1840
Mary Melvina Williams	17	Pulaski County	Pulaski County		Seamstress	27 Aug 1840
Ephragin Newsome	33	12 Sep 1810, Laurens County, about 12 miles from Tramel's Ferry	Pulaski County		Boat poler or farmer	5 Oct 1843
Penny Padget	36	1808 in North Carolina	Pulaski County		Washer woman & seamstress	7 Feb 1844
Betsey Williams	40	1804 in Burke County	Pulaski County		Washer &c	7 Feb 1844
Milley	21	1823 in Pulaski County	Pulaski County		Seamstress	7 Feb 1844
Michael Williams, a woman	16	1828 in Dooly County	Pulaski County		Seamstress	7 Feb 1844
Caroline Padget	11	1833 in Jefferson County	Pulaski County		Seamstress	7 Feb 1844
John General	30	1814 in Virginia	Wilkes County, then Oglethorpe County, now Pulaski	When quite small	Carpenter	8 Feb 1844

Name	Age	Place of Nativity	Residence	Time of Coming into Georgia	Occupation	Date
			County			
Dread Newsome	36	1818 in Burke County	Pulaski County		Boat [illegible]	21 Feb 1844
Loucinda Newsome	25	1819 in Emanuel County	Pulaski County		Seamstress	21 Feb 1844
Ephraigm Newsome	33	1810 Laurens County about 12 miles from Trammel's Ferry	Pulaski		Boat Pilot	25 Mar 1844
John Jones	42	1802 in South Carolina	Baldwin County, then Muscogee County, now Pulaski County	Unknown	Boat hand	18 Oct 1844
Joannah Durham	5	1842 in Houston County	With Jordan Scott in Pulaski County			6 Jan 1847
Jordan Scott	37	Martin County, North Carolina	Pulaski County	Unknown	Boatman	23 Feb 1847
Tempy Boon	32	1815 in Pulaski County	Hawkinsville		Seamstress	22 Feb 1847
Penny Padget	38	Sampson County, North	Pulaski County	Unknown	Washing &c	23 Feb

Name	Age	Place of Nativity	Residence	Time of Coming into Georgia	Occupation	Date
		Carolina				1847
Dread Newsome	31	1815 in Burke County	Pulaski County		Farmer & boat pilot	27 Feb 1847
Loucinda Newsome	28	1819 in Emanuel County	With husband Dread		Seamstress	27 Feb 1847
Olliff Thomas	54	North Carolina	Pulaski County		Farming & weaving	1 Mar 1847
Milley Williams	25	Pulaski County	Pulaski County		Seamstress & caner	1 Mar 1847
Wriley Williams	20		Pulaski County		Farming &c	1 Mar 1847
Elizabeth Williams	43	1804 in Burk County	Pulaski County		Washer &c	1 Mar 1847
Peggy Williams	50	Sampson County, North Carolina	Pulaski County	1810	Washing &c	1 Mar 1847
Michael Williams	19	1828 in Dooly County	Pulaski County		Seamstress	17 Mar 1847
Joseph Williams	16 or 17	Dooly County	Pulaski County		Farming &c	17 Mar 1847
Matilda Williams	18	Dooly County	Pulaski County		House servant	17 Mar 1847

Name	Age	Place of Nativity	Residence	Time of Coming into Georgia	Occupation	Date
Penny Padget	39	Sampson County, North Carolina	Pulaski County	Unknown	Washing &c	16 Feb 1848
Elizabeth Williams		1804 in Burke County	Pulaski County		Washing &c	16 Feb 1848
Michael Williams		1828 in Dooly County	Pulaski County		Seamstress	16 Feb 1848
Joseph Williams	17 or 18	Dolly County	Pulaski County		Faming &c	16 Feb 1848
Matilda Williams	18 or 19	Dooly County	Pulaski County		House servant	16 Feb 1848
Wriley Williams	19 or 20		Pulaski County		Boating & farming	16 Feb 1848
Milley	25	1823 in Pulaski County	Pulaski County		Seamstress	24 Feb 1848
Peggy Williams	51	Sampson County, North Carolina	Pulaski County	1810	Washing &c	24 Feb 1848
Tempy Boon	33	1815 in Pulaski County	Hawkinsville		Seamstress & washer	1 Mar 1848
Olliff Thomas	53	North Carolina	Pulaski County		Farming	26 Apr 1848

Name	Age	Place of Nativity	Residence	Time of Coming into Georgia	Occupation	Date
John Generals	36	Virginia	Wilkes County, now Pulaski County		Carpenter	26 Apr 1848
Dread Newsom	35	1813 in Burke County	Pulaski County		Farmer & boat pilot	27 Jul 1848
Lucindy Newsom, wife of Dread	28	1819 in Emanuel County	Pulaski County		Seamstress	27 Jul 1848
Penny Padget	40	Sampson County, North Carolina	Pulaski County		Wash woman	1 May 1849
Riley Williams	21	Dooly County	Pulaski County		Boat hand	1 May 1849
Dread Newsom	36	1813 in Burke County	Pulaski County		Farmer & boat pilot	29 Mar 1850
Lucindy Newsome	29	1819 in Emanuel County	With husband Dread in Pulaski County		Seamstress	29 Mar 1850
Riley Williams	22	Dooly County	Pulaski County		Boat hand	2 Apr 1850
Elizabeth Williams	46	1804 in Burke County	Pulaski County		Washer &c	3 Apr 1850

Name	Age	Place of Nativity	Residence	Time of Coming into Georgia	Occupation	Date
Penney Padget	41	Sampson County, North Carolina	Pulaski County	Unknown	Washer woman	2 Apr 1850
Evaline Williams	17	Jefferson County	Pulaski County		Seamstress	2 Apr 1850
Elizabeth Matilda Williams	16	Dooly County	Pulaski County		Seamstress	2 Apr 1850
Milley Williams	28	Pulaski County	Pulaski County		Seamstress	2 Apr 1850
Joe Williams	18 or 19	Dooly County	Pulaski County		Farmer	2 Apr 1850
Lourane Williams	9	Dooly County	Pulaski County			3 Apr 1850
Franklin Williams	8	Pulaski County	Pulaski County			3 Apr 1850
Riley Williams	24 or 25	Dooly County	Pulaski County		Boat hand	30 Apr 1853
Eveline Williams	20	Jefferson County	Pulaski County		Seamstress	30 Apr 1853
Penney Padget	44	Sampson County, North Carolina	Pulaski County	Unknown	Washer woman	30 Apr 1853

Name	Age	Place of Nativity	Residence	Time of Coming into Georgia	Occupation	Date
Peggy Williams	56	Sampson County, North Carolina	Pulaski County	1810	Washer	3 May 1853
Margarett Williams	9	Pulaski County	Pulaski County			3 May 1853
John Williams	8	Pulaski County	Pulaski County			3 May 1853
Elizabeth Williams		1804 Burke County	Pulaski County		Washer &	3 May 1853
Joseph Williams	21	1833 in Dooly County	Pulaski County		Farmer	3 May 1853
Louiza Williams	14	Pulaski County	Pulaski County			3 May 1853
Franklin Williams	10	Pulaski County	Pulaski County			3 May 1853
Molley Williams	30	Pulaski County	Pulaski County		Field hand	3 May 1853
Joe Williams	5	Pulaski County	Pulaski County			3 May 1853
William Williams	4	Pulaski County	Pulaski County			3 May 1853
Anaca	2	Pulaski	Pulaski			3

Name	Age	Place of Nativity	Residence	Time of Coming into Georgia	Occupation	Date
Williams		County	County			May 1853
Elin Williams	4	Pulaski County	Pulaski County			3 May 1853
Augustus Williams		Pulaski County	Pulaski County			3 May 1853
Matilda Williams		Dooly County	Pulaski County		House servant	3 May 1853
William McGlocklin			Pulaski County		Boat hand	3 May 1853
Olliff Thomas	64	Greene County, North Carolina	Pulaski County	When she was quite small	Farmer	14 May 1853
Ephragm Newsome		Laurens County	Pulaski County		Boatman	14 May 1853
Elizabeth Williams		1804 in Burke County	Pulaski County		Washer	18 Jan 1854
Joseph Williams	21	Dooly County	Pulaski County		Farmer	18 Jan 1854
Louisa Williams	15	Pulaski County	Pulaski County			18 Jan 1854
Frank Williams	11	Pulaski County	Pulaski County			18 Jan

Name	Age	Place of Nativity	Residence	Time of Coming into Georgia	Occupation	Date
						1854
[too faint]					Seamstress	2 Feb 1854
Margarett Williams	11	Pulaski County	With her mother Milley Williams in Pulaski County			2 Feb 1854
John Calvin Williams	9	Pulaski County	With his mother Milley in Pulaski County			2 Feb 1854
William Riley Williams	5	Pulaski County	With his mother Milley in Pulaski County			2 Feb 1854
Joseph Williams	3	Pulaski County	With his mother Milley in Pulaski County			2 Feb 1854
Aunaca Williams	2	Pulaski County	With her mother Milley in Pulaski County			2 Feb 1854
Matilda Williams	24	Dooly County	Pulaski County		House servant	2 Feb 1854

Name	Age	Place of Nativity	Residence	Time of Coming into Georgia	Occupation	Date
Peggy Williams	57	Sampson County, North Carolina	Pulaski County	1810	Washer	9 Feb 1854
Wriley Williams	25	Dooly County	Pulaski County		Boat hand	13 Mar 1854
Eveline Williams	21	Jefferson County	Pulaski County		Seamstress	13 Mar 1854
Olliff Thomas	65	Greene County, North Carolina	Pulaski County	When she was quite small	Tiller of the Earth	13 Mar 1854
Dread Newsom	40	1813 in Burke County	Pulaski County		Farmer & boat pilot	13 Mar 1854
Loucinda Newsom		1819 in Emanuel County	With husband Dread		seamstress	13 Mar 1854
Marin Newsom, son of Dread	19	Pulaski County	Pulaski County		teamster	13 Mar 1854
Dread Newsom, son of Dread		Pulaski County	Pulaski County			13 Mar 1854
Margarett Newsom, daughter of Dread		Pulaski County	Pulaski County			13 Mar 1854

Name	Age	Place of Nativity	Residence	Time of Coming into Georgia	Occupation	Date
Betsey Williams	55	Burke County	Pulaski County		Farmer. Asa Pipkin, Guardian	7 Feb 1855
Frank Williams	13	Pulaski County	Pulaski County		Asa Pipkin, Guardian	7 Feb 1855
Loui Newsom	16	West Florida	Pulaski County	When about 3 months old	Sempstress & washer	7 Feb 1854
Peggy Williams	60	Sampson County, North Carolina	Pulaski County	When about 8 years old	Sempstress & washer woman	7 Feb 1855
Matilda Williams	74	Dooly County	Pulaski County		Washer woman. Asa Pipkin, Guardian	7 Feb 1854
Mose Newsom	18	Pulaski County	Pulaski County		Wagoner & boat hand. Asa Pipkin, Guardian	12 Feb 1855
Clarasy J. Newsom	15	Macon, Bibb County	Came to Pulaski County about 8 months ago		Household affairs of herself & husband. John H. Wallace, Guardian	12 Feb 1855
Riley Williams	26	Dooly County	Pulaski County		Boat hand. Asa Pipkin, Guardian	12 Feb 1855
Eveline Williams, wife of	22	Jefferson County	Pulaski County		Sempstress. H. H. Hansell,	12 Feb

Name	Age	Place of Nativity	Residence	Time of Coming into Georgia	Occupation	Date
Riley					Guardian	1855
Penny Padget	55	Sampson County, North Carolina	Pulaski County	Unknown	Washer woman. H. H. Hansell, Guardian	1 Feb 1855
Milley Williams	30	Pulaski County	Pulaski County		Washer woman. H. H. Hansell, Guardian	1 Feb 1855
John Calvin, son of Milley Williams	10				John H. Wallace. Guardian	1 Feb 1855
William Riley, son of Milley Williams	8				Asa Pipkin, Guardian	1 Feb 1855
Joseph, son of Milley Williams	5					1 Feb 1855
Hunaca, daughter of Milley Williams	3					1 Feb 1855
Joseph Williams	23	Dooly County	Pulaski County		Farmer. Asa Pipkin, Guardian	4 Feb 1855
Dread Newsom	41	Burke County	Came to Pulaski County when quite		Boat pilot. John D. Gordon, Guardian	19 Feb 1855

134

Name	Age	Place of Nativity	Residence	Time of Coming into Georgia	Occupation	Date
			small			
Lucinda Newsom. Wife of Dread	37	Emanuel County	Pulaski County		Sempstress. Asa Pipkin, Guardian	19 Feb 1855
Margaret Ann Newsom, daughter of Dread	16	Pulaski County	With her parents in Pulaski County		Asa Pipkin, Guardian	19 Feb 1855
Dread Newsom, Jr., son of Dread	13	Pulaski County	With his parents in Pulaski County		Asa Pipkin, Guardian	19 Feb 1855
Jerry Boon, son of Tempy Boon	21	Pulaski County	Pulaski County		Farming. B. N. Mitchell, Guardian	25 Feb 1855
Jarret A. Newsome	38	Jefferson County	Pulaski County		Yellow complexion	23 Jul 1855
Ephram Newsome	50	Laurens County	Pulaski County		Farming & steamboat pilot. Joseph Caruthers, Guardian. Paid a fine of $100 as prescribed by law.	8 Aug 1855
Olliff Thomas	65	Greene County, North	Pulaski County	When quite small.	Farming & washer woman. Eli Shivers,	18 Aug 1855

Name	Age	Place of Nativity	Residence	Time of Coming into Georgia	Occupation	Date
		Carolina			Guardian. Paid fine of $100 for not registering according to law.	
Penny Padget	56	Sampson County, North Carolina	Pulaski County	Unknown	Washer woman. Dark complexion, stout built. A. H. Hansell, Guardian	1 Feb 1856
Milley Williams	31	Pulaski County	Pulaski County		Washer woman. A. H. Hansell, Guardian	1 Feb 1856
Margaret, daughter of Milley Williams	12	Pulaski County	Pulaski County			1 Feb 1856
John Calvin, son of Milley Williams		Pulaski County	Pulaski County			1 Feb 1856
William Riley, son of Milley Williams		Pulaski County	Pulaski County			1 Feb 1856
Joseph, son of Milley Williams		Pulaski County	Pulaski County			1 Feb 1856

Name	Age	Place of Nativity	Residence	Time of Coming into Georgia	Occupation	Date
Anackey, daughter of Milley Williams	4	Pulaski County	Pulaski County			1 Feb 1856
Joseph Williams	24	Dooly County	Pulaski County		Farmer & boatman. Yellow complexion. Asa Pipkin, Guardian	2 Feb 1856
Riley Williams	27	Dooly County	Pulaski County		Boat hand & engineer. Light yellow complexion. Asa Pipkin, Guardian	2 Feb 1856
Eveline Williams, wife of Riley	22	Jefferson County	Pulaski County		Seamstress. Light yellow complexion. A. H. Hansell, Guardian	2 Feb 1856
Louisa Newsom	16	West Florida	Pulaski County		Seamstress. Light yellow complexion. Asa Pipkin, Guardian	2 Feb 1856
Louisa, child of Louisa Newsom	2, next Apr					2 Feb 1856
Moses Newsom	19	Pulaski County	Pulaski County		Wagoner & boat hand. Asa Pipkin, Guardian	5 Feb 1856

Name	Age	Place of Nativity	Residence	Time of Coming into Georgia	Occupation	Date
Claisa Newsom, wife of Moses		Bibb County	Came to Pulaski County about 3 years ago		Seamstress. John H. Wallace, Guardian	5 Feb 1856
Ephram Newsom	51	Laurens County	Pulaski County		Farming & boat pilot. Dark complexion, stout built. W. S. Langmate, Guardian	15 Apr 1856
Jarret A. Newsom	39	Jefferson County	Pulaski County		Stout heavy built. Rather light complexion. W. S. Langmate, Guardian	15 Apr 1856
Betsey Williams	55	Burke County	Pulaski County		Farmer. Asa Pipkin, Guardian	15 Apr 1856
Frank Williams	14	Pulaski County	Pulaski County		Farming. Asa Pipkin, Guardian	15 Apr 1856
Peggy Williams	61	Sampson County, North Carolina	Pulaski County	When about 8 years old	Seamstress & washer woman. Asa Pipkin, Guardian	15 Apr 1856
Matilda Williams	25	Dooly County	Pulaski County		Seamstress & washer woman. Asa Pipkin,	7 Jun 1856

Name	Age	Place of Nativity	Residence	Time of Coming into Georgia	Occupation	Date
					Guardian	
Dread Newsom	42	Burke County	Came to Pulaski County when quite small		Farmer & boat pilot. John D. Gordon, Guardian	7 Jun 1856
Lucinda Newsom, wife of Dread	38	Emanuel County	Pulaski County		Seamstress. Asa Pipkin, Guardian	7 Jun 1856
Margaret Ann Newsom, daughter of Dread	17	Pulaski County	Pulaski County		Washer. Asa Pipkin, Guardian	7 Jun 1856
Dread Newsom, Jr., son of Dread	14	Pulaski County	Pulaski County		Yellow complexion. Asa Pipkin, Guardian	7 Jun 1856
Biddy Bradshaw	27	Pulaski County	Pulaski County		Washing & seamstress. Light complexion. Without a guardian	23 Jul 1856
Penny Padget	57	Sampson County, North Carolina	Pulaski County		Washing. Dark complexion, stout built. A. H. Hansell, Guardian	7 May 1857
Milley Williams	32	Pulaski County	Pulaski County		Washing &c Dark complexion,	7 May

139

Name	Age	Place of Nativity	Residence	Time of Coming into Georgia	Occupation	Date
					slender built. A. H. Hansell, Guardian	1857
Margaret Williams, daughter of Milley	12	Pulaski County	Pulaski County		A. H. Hansell, of Thomas County, Guardian	
John Calvin Williams, son of Milley		Pulaski County	Pulaski County		A. H. Hansell, of Thomas County, Guardian	
William Riley Williams, son of Milley		Pulaski County	Pulaski County		A. H. Hansell, of Thomas County, Guardian	
Joseph Williams, son of Milley		Pulaski County	Pulaski County		A. H. Hansell, of Thomas County, Guardian	
Anakey Williams, daughter of Milley		Pulaski County	Pulaski County		A. H. Hansell, of Thomas County, Guardian	
Oliff Williams, daughter of Milley	1	Pulaski County	Pulaski County		A. H. Hansell, of Thomas County, Guardian	

Name	Age	Place of Nativity	Residence	Time of Coming into Georgia	Occupation	Date
Peggy Williams	62	Sampson County, North Carolina	Pulaski County	When about 8 years old	Washing & seamstress. Yellow complexion, low stout built. Alexander Pipken, Guardian	7 May 1857
Betsey Williams	55	Burke County	Pulaski County		Farming. Light complexion. Warren D. Wood, Guardian	29 Jun 1857
Frank Williams	15	Pulaski County	Pulaski County		Farming. Yellow complexion. Warren D. Wood	29 Jun 1857
Joseph Williams	24	Dooly County	Pulaski County		Farmer & boat hand. Yellow complexion. Warren D. Wood Guardian	1 Jul 1857
Ephraim Newsom	52	Laurens County	Pulaski County		Farming & boat pilot. Stout built, dark complexion. Joseph Carruthers, Guardian	8 Jul 1857
Biddy	28	Pulaski	Pulaski		Washing & seamstress.	8 Jul

Name	Age	Place of Nativity	Residence	Time of Coming into Georgia	Occupation	Date
Bradshaw		County	County		Light yellow complexion	1857
Milley Williams	33	Pulaski County	Pulaski County		Washing &c Dark complexion, rather slender built. A. H. Hansell, of Thomas County, Guardian	15 Feb 1858
Margaret Williams, daughter of Milley	13	Pulaski County	Pulaski County		A. H. Hansell, of Thomas County, Guardian	15 Feb 1858
John Calvin Williams, son of Milley	12	Pulaski County	Pulaski County		A. H. Hansell, of Thomas County, Guardian	15 Feb 1858
William Riley Williams, son of Milley	9	Pulaski County	Pulaski County		A. H. Hansell, of Thomas County, Guardian	15 Feb 1858
Joseph Williams, son of Milley	8	Pulaski County	Pulaski County		A. H. Hansell, of Thomas County, Guardian	15 Feb 1858
Anaky Williams, daughter of	7	Pulaski County	Pulaski County		A. H. Hansell, of Thomas	15 Feb

Name	Age	Place of Nativity	Residence	Time of Coming into Georgia	Occupation	Date
Milley					County, Guardian	1858
Oliff Williams, daughter of Milley	2	Pulaski County	Pulaski County		A. H. Hansell, of Thomas County, Guardian	15 Feb 1858
Penny Padget	58	Sampson County, North Carolina	Pulaski County		Washing &c Dark complexion, stout built. A. H. Hansell, Guardian	15 Feb 1858
Riley Williams	29	Dooly County	Pulaski County		Engineer boatman. Light complexion, small size. A. H. Hansell, Guardian	15 Feb 1858
Eveline Williams, wife of Riley	22	Jefferson County	Pulaski County		Seamstress. Light yellow complexion. A. H. Hansell, Guardian	15 Feb 1858
Joseph Williams	26	Dooly County	Pulaski County		Boat hand. Yellow complexion, weighs about 160 or 170 pounds. Warren D. Wood,	15 Feb 1858

Name	Age	Place of Nativity	Residence	Time of Coming into Georgia	Occupation	Date
					Guardian	
Michael Williams	30	Dooly County	Pulaski County		Seamstress. A. C. Bostrick, Guardian	15 Feb 1858
Betsey Williams	56	Burke County	Pulaski County		Farming. Light complexion. W. D. Wood, Guardian	6 Apr 1858
Frank Williams	16	Pulaski County	Pulaski County		Farming. Light yellow complexion. W. D. Wood Guardian	6 Apr 1858
Matilda Williams	27	Dooly County	Pulaski County		Washing & seamstress. Light complexion.	6 Apr 1858
Ephraim Newsom	53	Laurens County	Pulaski County		Farming & boat pilot. Stout built, dark complexion. Joseph Carruthers, Guardian	23 Apr 1858
Wesley Waters	20	Pulaski County	Pulaski County		Farmer. Yellow complexion. W. D. Wood, Guardian	8 Jul 1858

Name	Age	Place of Nativity	Residence	Time of Coming into Georgia	Occupation	Date
Milley Williams	34	Pulaski County	Pulaski County		Washing &c Dark complexion, rather slender built. A. H. Hansell, of Thomas County, Guardian	1 Feb 1859
Margaret Williams, daughter of Milley	14	Pulaski County	Pulaski County		A. H. Hansell, of Thomas County, Guardian	1 Feb 1859
John Calvin Williams, son of Milley	13	Pulaski County	Pulaski County		A. H. Hansell, of Thomas County, Guardian	1 Feb 1859
William Riley Williams, son of Milley	10	Pulaski County	Pulaski County		A. H. Hansel,l of Thomas County, Guardian	1 Feb 1859
Joseph Williams, son of Milley	9	Pulaski County	Pulaski County		A. H. Hansell, of Thomas County, Guardian	1 Feb 1859
Anaky Williams, daughter of Milley	8	Pulaski County	Pulaski County		A. H. Hansell, of Thomas County, Guardian	1 Feb 1859

Name	Age	Place of Nativity	Residence	Time of Coming into Georgia	Occupation	Date
Olliff Williams, daughter of Milley	3	Pulaski County	Pulaski County		A. H. Hansell, of Thomas County, Guardian	1 Feb 1859
Michael Williams	30	Dooly County	Pulaski County		Seamstress. Light complexion. A. C. Bostrick, Guardian	1 Feb 1859
Eveline Williams, wife of Riley	23	Jefferson County	Pulaski County		Seamstress &c. Light yellow complexion. A. H. Hansell, Guardian	14 Feb 1859
Riley Williams	30	Dooly County	Pulaski County		Engineer & boatman. Light complexion, small size. A. H. Hansell, Guardian	14 Feb 1859
Penny Padget	59	Sampson County, North Carolina	Pulaski County		Washing &c Dark complexion, stout built. A. H. Hansell, Guardian	14 Feb 1859
Betsey Williams	61	Burke County	Pulaski County		Farming &c Light complexion. Warren D.	16 Mar 1859

Name	Age	Place of Nativity	Residence	Time of Coming into Georgia	Occupation	Date
					Wood, Guardian	
Frank Williams	16	Pulaski County	Pulaski County		Farming. Light yellow complexion. W. D. Wood, Guardian	16 Mar 1859
Matilda Williams	28	Dooly County	Pulaski County		Washing & seamstress. Light complexion	18 Mar 1859
Wesley Waters	22	Pulaski County	Pulaski County		Striker in blacksmith shop. Yellow complexion. W. D. Wood, Guardian	21 Jun 1859
Ephaim Newsom	53	Laurens County	Pulaski County		Boat pilot. Stout built, dark complexion. Joseph Carruthers, Guardians	27 Jul 1859
Joseph Williams	27	Dooly County	Pulaski County		Boat hand. Yellow complexion. Warren D. Wood, Guardian	27 Jul 1859
Penny Padget	60	Sampson County, North	Pulaski County		Washing &c Dark complexion,	17 Jan

Name	Age	Place of Nativity	Residence	Time of Coming into Georgia	Occupation	Date
		Carolina			stout built. John H. Walter, Guardian	1860
Evaline Williams	24	Jefferson County	Pulaski County		Seamstress &c. Yellow complexion, stout built. A. H. Hansell, Guardian	24 Jan 1860
Milly Williams	35	Pulaski County	Pulaski County		Washing &c Dark complexion, rather slender built. A. H. Hansell, Guardian	24 Jan 1860
Margaret Williams, daughter of Milly	15	Pulaski County	Pulaski County		A. H. Hansell, Guardian	24 Jan 1860
John C. Williams, son of Milly	14	Pulaski County	Pulaski County		A. H. Hansell, Guardian	24 Jan 1860
Joseph Williams, son of Milly	10	Pulaski County	Pulaski County		A. H. Hansell, Guardian	24 Jan 1860
Amaky Williams, daughter of Milly	9	Pulaski County	Pulaski County		A. H. Hansell, Guardian	24 Jan 1860

Name	Age	Place of Nativity	Residence	Time of Coming into Georgia	Occupation	Date
Oliff Williams, daughter of Milly	4	Pulaski County	Pulaski County		A. H. Hansell, Guardian	24 Jan 1860
Thomas Williams, son of Milly	8 mos.	Pulaski County	Pulaski County		A. H. Hansell, Guardian	24 Jan 1860
Betsey Williams	62	Burke County	Pulaski County		Farming. Light complexion. W. D. Wood, Guardian	9 Feb 1860
Franklin Williams	18	Pulaski County	Pulaski County		Farming. Light yellow complexion. W. D. Wood, Guardian	9 Feb 1860
Matilda Williams	29	Dooly County	Pulaski County		Washing & seamstress. Light complexion	9 Feb 1860
Marshall Meghee	34	Pulaski County	Pulaski County		Carpenter. Light complexion. Augustin Hansell, Guardian	10 Feb 1860
Cornelia Elizabeth Meghee	28	Pulaski County	Pulaski County		Seamstress. Light complexion. Augustin Hansell, Guardian	10 Feb 1860

Name	Age	Place of Nativity	Residence	Time of Coming into Georgia	Occupation	Date
Matilda Meghee	63	Richmond County	Pulaski County		Seamstress. Light complexion. Augustin Hansell, Guardian	10 Feb 1860
Michael Williams	31	Dooly County	Pulaski County		Seamstress. Light complexion. A. C. Bostick, Guardian	13 Feb 1860
Adam Mcghee	25		Pulaski County		Carpenter & boat hand. Light complexion	20 July 1860
Ephraim Newsom	54	Laurens County	Pulaski County		Boat pilot. Stout built, dark complexion. Joseph Carruthers, Guardian	23 Jul 1860
Penny Padget	61	Sampson County, North Carolina	Pulaski County		Washing &c Dark complexion, stout built. John H. Wallace, Guardian	28 Mar 1861
Evaline Williams	26	Jefferson County	Pulaski County		Seamstress &c. Yellow complexion, stout built. A. H. Hansell,	28 Mar 1861

Name	Age	Place of Nativity	Residence	Time of Coming into Georgia	Occupation	Date
					Guardian	
Milley Williams	36	Pulaski County	Pulaski County		Washing. Dark complexion, rather slender built. A. H. Hansell, Guardian	28 Mar 1861
Margaret Williams, daughter of Milley	16	Pulaski County	Pulaski County		A. H. Hansell, Guardian	28 Mar 1861
John C. Williams, son of Milley	15	Pulaski County	Pulaski County		A. H. Hansell, Guardian	28 Mar 1861
Joseph Williams, son of Milley	11	Pulaski County	Pulaski County		A. H. Hansell, Guardian	28 Mar 1861
Arnaky Williams, daughter of Milley	10	Pulaski County	Pulaski County		A. H. Hansell, Guardian	28 Mar 1861
Oliff Williams, daughter of Milley	4	Pulaski County	Pulaski County		A. H. Hansell, Guardian	28 Mar 1861
Thomas Williams, son of Milley	1 year, 8 mos.	Pulaski County	Pulaski County		A. H. Hansell, Guardian	28 Mar 1861

Name	Age	Place of Nativity	Residence	Time of Coming into Georgia	Occupation	Date
Betsy Williams	63	Burke County	Pulaski County		Farming. Light complexion. W. D. Wood, Guardian	28 Mar 1861
Franklin Williams	19	Pulaski County	Pulaski County		Farming. Light yellow complexion. W. D. Wood, Guardian	28 Mar 1861
Matilda Williams	30	Dooly County	Pulaski County		Washing & seamstress. Light complexion	28 Mar 1861
Ephram Newsom	55	Laurens County	Pulaski County		Boat pilot. Stout built, dark complexion. Joseph Carruthers, Guardian	13 Apr 1861
Michael Williams	32	Dooly County	Pulaski County		Seamstress. Light complexion. A. C. Bostick, Guardian	16 Apr 1861
Adam Mcghee	26		Pulaski County		Carpenter or boat hand. Light Complexion	16 Apr 1861
Ann Williams	22		Pulaski County		Washing. Dark	15 May

Name	Age	Place of Nativity	Residence	Time of Coming into Georgia	Occupation	Date
					complexion	1861
Marshall Mcghee	35	Pulaski County	Pulaski County		Carpenter. Light complexion. Aug. H. Hansell, Guardian	1 Jun 1861
Cornelia Elizabeth Mcghee	29	Pulaski County	Pulaski County		Seamstress. Light complexion. Aug. H. Hansell, Guardian	1 Jun 1861
Matilda Mcghee	64	Richmond County	Pulaski County		Seamstress. Light complexion. Aug. H. Hansell, Guardian	1 Jun 1861
Milla Williams	37	Pulaski County	Pulaski County		Dark complexion. Aug. H. Hansell, Guardian	29 Apr 1862
Margaret Williams, daughter of Milla	17	Pulaski County	Pulaski County		Aug. H. Hansell, Guardian	29 Apr 1862
John C. Williams, son of Milla	16	Pulaski County	Pulaski County		Aug. H. Hansell, Guardian	29 Apr 1862
Joseph Williams, son of Milla	14	Pulaski County	Pulaski County		Aug. H. Hansell, Guardian	29 Apr 1862

Name	Age	Place of Nativity	Residence	Time of Coming into Georgia	Occupation	Date
Milla Williams, daughter of Milla	15	Pulaski County	Pulaski County		Aug. H. Hansell, Guardian	29 Apr 1862
Evaline Williams	30	Jefferson County	Pulaski County		Seamstress. Yellow complexion. Aug. H. Hansell, Guardian	29 Apr 1862
Lugerly Williams	14	Pulaski County	Pulaski County		Aug. H. Hansell, Guardian	29 Apr 1862
Penny Padget	62	Sampson County, North Carolina	Pulaski County		Washing. Dark complexion, stout built. John H. Wallace, Guardian	29 Apr 1862
Michael Williams	31	Dooly County	Pulaski County		Seamstress. Light complexion. A. C. Bostick, Guardian	29 Apr 1862
Betsey Williams	63	Burke County	Pulaski County		Farming. Light complexion. W. D. Wood, Guardian	29 Apr 1862
Matilda Williams	30	Dooly County	Pulaski County		Cook. Light complexion. W. D. Wood,	29 Apr 1862

Name	Age	Place of Nativity	Residence	Time of Coming into Georgia	Occupation	Date
					Guardian	
Franklin Williams	19	Pulaski County	Pulaski County		Farming. Light complexion. W. D. Wood, Guardian	29 Apr 1862
Ephriam Williams	38	Laurens County	Pulaski County		Boat pilot. Dark complexion. Joseph Carruthers, Guardian	30 Apr 1862
Marshall McGhee	36		Pulaski County		A. H. Hansell, Guardian, of Thomasville	
Adam McGhee	27		Pulaski County		A. H. Hansell, Guardian, of Thomasville	
Matilda McGhee	65		Pulaski County		A. H. Hansell, Guardian, of Thomasville	
Cornelia Elizabeth McGhee	30		Pulaski County		A. H. Hansell, Guardian, of Thomasville	
Wesley Walters	24	Pulaski County	Pulaski County		Blacksmith. Yellow complexion. W. D. Wood,	13 Dec 1862

Name	Age	Place of Nativity	Residence	Time of Coming into Georgia	Occupation	Date
					Guardian	
Moses Powel	45	Richmond County	Pulaski County		Carpenter. Capes color, 5 feet 9 inches tall. C. M. Bozeman, Guardian	9 Jan 1863
Milley Williams	38	Pulaski County	Pulaski County		Washing. Dark complexion. A. H. Hansell, Guardian	11 Feb 1863
John C. Williams, son of Milley	17	Pulaski County	Pulaski County		Yellow complexion. A. H. Hansell, Guardian	11 Feb 1863
William Williams, son of Milley	16	Pulaski County	Pulaski County		Dark complexion. A. H. Hansell, Guardian	11 Feb 1863
Wesley Waters	24	Pulaski County	Pulaski County		Blacksmith. Yellow complexion. W. D. Wood	11 Feb 1863
Margaret Waters, wife of Wesley	18	Pulaski County	Pulaski County		Washing & ironing. Yellow complexion. W. D. Wood, Guardian	11 Feb 1863

Name	Age	Place of Nativity	Residence	Time of Coming into Georgia	Occupation	Date
Betsey Williams	64	Burke County	Pulaski County		Farming. Light complexion. W. D. Wood, Guardian	10 Mar 1863
Franklin Williams	26	Pulaski County	Pulaski County		Farming. Light complexion. W. D. Wood, Guardian	2 Mar 1863
Matilda Williams	31	Dooly County	Pulaski County		Cook. Light complexion. W. D. Wood, Guardian	2 Mar 1863
Ephram Newsom	59	Laurens County	Pulaski county		Boat pilot. Dark complexion. Joseph Carruthers, Guardian	4 Apr 1863
Ann Williams	26		Pulaski County		Washing & ironing. Dark complexion	4 Apr 1863
Anderson Newsom	32	Pulaski County	Pulaski County		Boat pilot. Dark complexion. Joseph Carruthers, Guardian	4 Apr 1863
Eveline Williams	31	Jefferson County	Pulaski County		Washer. Yellow complexion.	14 Apr

Name	Age	Place of Nativity	Residence	Time of Coming into Georgia	Occupation	Date
					John H. Wallier, Guardian	1863
Michael Williams	32	Dooly County	Pulaski County		Seamstress. Light complexion. A. C. Bostick, Guardian	3 Jun 1863
Marsel McGee	41		Pulaski County		Carpenter. Light complexion. A. H. Hansell, of Thomas County, Guardian	5 Jun 1863
Adam McGee	28		Pulaski County		Laborer. Light complexion. A. H. Hansell, of Thomas County, Guardian	5 Jun 1863
Matilda McGee	66	Virginia	Pulaski County		Seamstress. Light complexion. A. H. Hansell, of Thomas County, Guardian	5 Jun 1863
Cornelia Elizabeth McGee	31		Pulaski County		Seamstress. Light complexion. A. H.	5 Jun 1863

Name	Age	Place of Nativity	Residence	Time of Coming into Georgia	Occupation	Date
					Hansell, of Thomas County, Guardian	
Feriby Newsom	58	Pulaski County	Pulaski County		Laborer. Dark complexion. Joseph Carruthers, Guardian	6 Jul 1863
Milly Williams	39	Pulaski County	Pulaski County		Seamstress. Dark complexion. James S. Leith, Guardian	13 Feb 1864
John Williams, son of Milly	18	Pulaski County	Pulaski County		Yellow complexion. James S. Leith, Guardian	13 Feb 1864
William Williams, son of Milly		Pulaski County	Pulaski County		Dark complexion. James S. Leith, Guardian	13 Feb 1864
Westley Waters	25	Pulaski County	Pulaski County		Boating. Yellow complexion, 5 feet 10 inches tall. James S. Leith, Guardian	13 Feb 1864
Margarett Waters,	19		Pulaski		Washing & ironing.	13 Feb

Name	Age	Place of Nativity	Residence	Time of Coming into Georgia	Occupation	Date
wife of Westley			County		Yellow complexion. James S. Leith, Guardian	1864
Charles Waters, son of Westley	4 mos.	Pulaski County	Pulaski County		James S. Leith, Guardian	13 Feb 1864
Michael Williams	33	Dooly County	Pulaski County		Seamstress. Light complexion. Alfred C. Bosick, Guardian	16 Feb 1864
Adam McGhee	38	Pulaski County	Pulaski County			
Marshall McGhee	42	Pulaski County	Pulaski County			
Matilda McGhee	67	Virginia	Pulaski County			
Cornelia Elizabeth McGhee	32	Pulaski County	Pulaski County			
Eveline Williams	32	Jefferson County	Pulaski County		Seamstress. Light yellow complexion. Jeff Brown, Guardian	3 May 1864
Ephraim Newsom	60	Laurens County	Pulaski County		Boat pilot. Joseph Carruthers, Guardian	4 Jun 1864

Name	Age	Place of Nativity	Residence	Time of Coming into Georgia	Occupation	Date
Pheriba Newsom	59	Pulaski County	Pulaski County		Laborer. Dark complexion. Joseph Carruthers, Guardian	4 Jun 1864
Matilda Williams	32	Dooly County	Pulaski County		Cook. Light complexion. No guardian	29 Jun 1864
Betsey Williams	65	Burke County	Pulaski County		Farming. Light complexion. No guardian	29 Jun 1864
Franklin Williams	21	Pulaski County	Pulaski County		Farming. Light complexion. No guardian	29 Jun 1864
Milley Williams	40	Pulaski County	Pulaski County		Seamstress. Dark complexion. James S. Leith, Guardian	13 Feb 1865
John Williams, son of Milley	18	Pulaski County	Pulaski County		Yellow complexion. James S. Leith, Guardian	13 Feb 1865
William Williams, son of Milley	17	Pulaski County	Pulaski County		Dark complexion. James S. Leith, Guardian	13 Feb 1865
Michael	34	Dooly	Pulaski		Seamstress. Light	13 Feb

Name	Age	Place of Nativity	Residence	Time of Coming into Georgia	Occupation	Date
Williams		County	County		complexion. A. C. Bostick, Guardian	1865
Wesley Waters	26	Pulaski County	Pulaski County		Boating. Yellow complexion, 5 feet 10 inches tall. James S. Leith, Guardian	13 Feb 1865
Margaret Waters, wife of Wesley	20	Pulaski County	Pulaski County		Washing & ironing. Yellow complexion. James S. Leith, Guardian	13 Feb 1865
Eveline Newsom	33	Jefferson County	Pulaski County		Seamstress. Light yellow complexion. Jeff Brown, Guardian	2 Aug 1865

Wilkes County

Clerks entered registrations in two different books held by the Court of Ordinary in Washington, Georgia, copies of both microfilm reels available in the microfilm reading room of the Georgia Department of Archives and History in Morrow, Georgia. The cover of the first register reads

Wilkes County
Register – Free Persons of Color
1819-1824

The clerk entered each registration in a paragraph format. The first entry reads

> February 20th 1Billy, a free man of Color, generally known by the name of Billy Honey has this day Entered his Name in Conformity to the law of this State. He states himself to be about 28 years of age and born in Chatham County and by Occupation a house carpenter. A Resident of Washington, Wilkes County. Certificate issued.

The following table presents the relevant information extracted from the original record.

Name	Age	Nativity	Residence	Occupation	Date
Billy Honey	28	Chatham County	Washington	House carpenter	20 Feb 1819
Gabriel Todd	60	North Carolina	Wilkes County	Masonik	20 Feb 1819
Patience Todd, wife of Gabriel	40	Virginia	Wilkes County		20 Feb 1819
Gabriel, child of Patience Todd	2	Georgia	Wilkes County		20 Feb 1819
Gloster Botts	24	Virginia	Washington	Carriage maker	27 Feb 1819
Patty Norman	37	Granville County, Virginia	Washington. Daughter Amey resides in Franklin County		27 Feb 1819
Susan Norman, child of Patty Nornman	19		Wilkes County		27 Feb 1819
Reubin Norman, child of Patty Norman	15		Franklin County		27 Feb 1819
Robert Norman, child of Patty Norman	14		Wilkes County		27 Feb 1819
Jesse Norman, child of Patty Norman	10		Wilkes County		27 Feb 1819
Wilis Norman, child of Patty	8		Milledgeville		27 Feb

Name	Age	Nativity	Residence	Occupation	Date
Norman					1819
Eliza Norman, child of Patty Norman	6		Wilkes County		27 Feb 1819
Paralle Norman, child of Patty Norman	3		Wilkes County		27 Feb 1819
Nancy Man	40	Louisa County, Virginia	Washington		27 Feb 1819
Sally Man	32	Wilkes County	Washington		27 Feb 1819
Peggy Wingfield	60	Hanover County, Virginia	Wilkes County		1 Mar 1819
Lennard Walden Corben	51	Halifax County, North Carolina	Wilkes County		1 Mar 1819
Robert	13	Elbert County	Wilkes County		1 Mar 1819
Malissa Man, daughter of Sally Man	14 or 15	Wilkes County	Wilkes County		1 Mar 1819
Mary Oliver	57	Lancaster County, Virginia	Wilkes County		1 Mar 1819
Dilsey	70	Amelia County, Virginia	Wilkes County		1 Mar 1819
Patty Norman	38	Granville County,	Wilkes County	Wash woman	17 Feb

Name	Age	Nativity	Residence	Occupation	Date
		Virginia			1820
Eliza, daughter of Patty Norman			Minor, living with mother.		17 Feb 1820
Paralle, daughter of Patty Norman			Minor, living with mother.		17 Feb 1820
Augustus, son of Patty Norman			Minor, living with mother.		17 Feb 1820
Malicy Mann	15 or 16	Wilkes County	Wilkes County		19 Feb 1820
Nancy Man	41	Louisa County, Virginia	Wilkes County		19 Feb 1820
Gloster Botts	25	Virginia	Wilkes County	Carpenter	27 Feb 1820
Peggy Wingfield	61	Hanover County, Virginia	Washington	Cook	19 Feb 1820
Dilcey	71	Amelia County, Virginia	Wilkes County	Cake woman	19 Feb 1820
Mary Oliver	58	Lancaster County, Virginia	Wilkes County		19 Feb 1820
Patience Todd	42	Louisa County, Virginia	Wilkes County	Cake woman	19 Feb 1819
Gabriel, son of Dicey	3	Richmond County	Wilkes County		19 Feb 1820

Name	Age	Nativity	Residence	Occupation	Date
Gabriel Todd	61	North Carolina	Wilkes County	Preacher	19 Feb 1820
Jinny Grant	33	Wilkes County	Wilkes County		21 Feb 1820
Billy Honey	29	Chatham County	Wilkes County	Carpenter	21 Feb 1820
Lusany Honey, wife of Billy	18	Columbia County	Wilkes County		21 Feb 1820
Valentine Sherrell	40	Columbia County	Wilkes County	Farmer	26 Feb 1820
Ambrose Perry	33	Orange County, Virginia	Wilkes County	Farmer	28 Feb 1820
Lewis Shops	25	Hancock County	Wilkes County	Blacksmith	29 Feb 1820
Newman Grant	37	Granville County, North Carolina	Wilkes County	Wagoner	11 Mar 1820
Leonard Walden Corbin	52	Halifax County, North Carolina	Wilkes County		27 Mar 1820
Thomas Boze	45	Culpepper County, Virginia	Wilkes County	Farmer	30 Mar 1820
Lewis Fields	18	Wilkes County	Wilkes County	Farmer	23 Jun 1820

Name	Age	Nativity	Residence	Occupation	Date
Euphusena Morris	55	Santo Domingo	Wilkes County	House woman	3 July 1820
Billy Honey	30	Chatham County	Wilkes County	Carpenter	13 Feb 1821
Lusaney Honey	19	Columbia County	Wilkes County		13 Feb 1821
Newman Grant	38	Granville County, North Carolina	Wilkes County		22 Feb 1821
Patty Norman	39	Granville County, Virginia	Wilkes County	Wash woman	
Eliza, daughter of Patty Norman	9	Elbert County	Wilkes County		
Paralle, daughter of Patty Norman	7	Wilkes County	Wilkes County		
Augustus Norman	2	Wilkes County	Wilkes County		
George	31	Formerly owned by Thomas Grant	Wilkes County	Farmer	6 Feb 1822
Fanny Sherrell	35		Wilkes County	Cook	18 Feb 1822
Melicy Man	16	Wilkes County	Wilkes County	Spinner & weaver	4 Mar 1822
Newman Grant	39		Wilkes County	Wagoner	12 Mar

Name	Age	Nativity	Residence	Occupation	Date
					1822
Jock Nelson	40	Brunswick County, Virginia	Wilkes County	Shoemaker	3 May 1822
Jenny Nelson	60	Harford County, Maryland	Wilkes County	Farmer	
Lewis Shops	27	Clarke County	Wilkes County	Blacksmith	27 Apr 1822
Ambrose	35	Orange County, Virginia	Wilkes County	Farmer	27 Apr 1822
Isham Scott	21	Johnson County, North Carolina	Wilkes County	Farmer	17 Jun 1822
Sally Man	31	Wilkes County	Wilkes County	Cook	18 Jun 1822
Gabriel Todd	63	North Carolina	Wilkes County	Preacher of the Gospel & farmer	18 Jun 1822
Patience Todd, wife of Gabriel	51	Virginia	Wilkes County	Baker	18 Jun 1822
Gabriel Todd, son of Patience Todd	5		Wilkes County		18 Jun 1822
Margaret Todd, daughter of Patience Todd	1		Wilkes County		18 Jun 1822
Lucinda Grant	41	Virginia	Wilkes County	Cook & washer	27 Jun

Name	Age	Nativity	Residence	Occupation	Date
					1822
David Grant, son of Lucinda Grant	15	Wilkes County	Wilkes County		27 Jun 1822
Dilsey Man	70	Amelia County, Virginia	Wilkes County	Barker	18 Jun 1822
Nancy Man	45	Virginia	Wilkes County	Baker	27 Jun 1822
Barbell Grant	31	Wilkes County	Wilkes County	Shoemaker	27 Feb 1823
Jock Nelson	41	Brunswick County, Virginia	Wilkes County	Shoemaker	4 Mar 1823
Thomas Boze	47	Born in Virginia, raised in Oglethorpe County	Wilkes County	Farmer	25 Feb 1823
Jenney Grant	35	Wilkes County	Wilkes County	Weaver	1 Apr 1823
Nancy Man	45	Virginia	Wilkes County	Baker	1 Apr 1823
Malicy Man	17	Wilkes County	Wilkes County	Spinner & weaver	1 Apr 1823
Delpha Denny	19	North Carolina	Wilkes County	Cook & spinner. John McCord, Guardian	

Name	Age	Nativity	Residence	Occupation	Date
Mary Valentine	27	Lunenburg County, Virginia	Wilkes County	Cook & washer	1 Apr 1823
Lewis Shops	28	Clarke County	Wilkes County	Blacksmith	26 Apr 1823
Ambrose Jerry	36	Orange County, Virginia	Wilkes County	Farmer	26 Feb 1823
Delsey Man	71	Amelia County, Virginia	Wilkes County	Baker	1 May 1823
Ambrose Jerry	36	Orange County, Virginia	Wilkes County	Farmer	19 Feb 1824
Daniel Moss	25	Greene County	Wilkes County	Farmer	21 Jan 1824
Lewis Shops	29	Clarke County	Wilkes County	Blacksmith	30 April 1824
Elise	22	North Carolina	Wilkes County	Spinning	4 May 1824

The cover of the second register reads

Wilkes County
Free Persons of Color - Estrays
1823-1826

The clerk entered each registration in a paragraph format. The first entry reads

February 25th 1825
A List of Free persons of Color

Georgia   }
Wilkes County   } Thomas Boze a Man of Color has this day entered his name
in this office as a free man of Color. Now about forty nine years of age & was
born in the State of Virginia and raised in the County of Oglethorpe, Georgia, and
now a resident of the County of Wilkes, and by occupation a farmer.

The following table presents the relevant information extracted from the eight registrations in the
original record. The estrays and other records in the book are not repeated here.

Name	Age	Nativity	Residence	Occupation	Date
Thomas Boze	49	Born in Virginia, raised in Oglethorpe County	Wilkes County	Farmer	25 Feb 1825
Barttell	33	Wilkes County	Wilkes County	Shoemaker	27 Feb 1825
Jack Nelson	43	Brunswick County, Virginia	Wilkes County	Shoemaker	4 Mar 1825
Malicy Man	19	Wilkes County	Wilkes County	Spinner & weaver	28 Mar 1825
Lewis Shops	30	Clarke County	Wilkes County	Blacksmith	30 Apr 1825
Allen Franklin	21	Wilkes County	Wilkes County	Farmer	17 Jul 1825
Barttell Grant	34	Wilkes County	Wilkes County	Shoemaker	3 Jan 1826
Lewis Sharp	31	Clarke County	Wilkes County	Blacksmith	30 Apr 1826

Index

Anderson
  John, 110
Arggerett
  George, 46
  John, 46
  Rosaline, 47
Bacon
  Eugene, 11
Baird
  Amey, 45, 48
  Charles, 44, 47, 55
  Henry, 44, 47, 52
  James, 48
  John, 45, 48
  Mary, 44, 47, 48
  Norris, 45, 48
  Polly, 44, 47
  Sipio, 44, 47, 52, 55
  William, 45, 47
  Willson, 44, 47
Barrett
  J. W., 64
Barrot, 9
  Betty, 9
  Lucy, 9
Bass
  Green, 60
  Grunel, 60
Benefield
  James, 115
  Madison, 112, 113
Bird
  Eliza, 108, 109
  John, 108, 109, 122
  Laura Antoinette, 109
  Margaret A., 109
  Margaret Ann, 108
  Martha A., 109
  Martha Ann, 108
Blont
  James C., 113
Boon
  Jerry, 135
  Tempy, 124, 126, 135
Bosick
  Alfred C., 160

Bostick
  A. C., 150, 152, 154, 158, 161
Bostrick
  A. C., 144, 146
Botts
  Gloster, 164, 166
Boze, 173
  Thomas, 167, 170, 172
Bozeman
  C. M., 156
Bradshaw
  Biddy, 139, 141
Braswell
  Milly, 99
Brewer
  Alonzo, 52, 55
  Edward, 55
  Edwin, 52
  Eliza, 55
  Elizabeth, 51, 54
  Georgia Ann, 51, 55
  Julia Ann, 55
Brickell
  John, 29, 35
  Wyley, 24, 29, 35
Brinson
  A. C., 87, 88, 91, 92
  Alexander, 70, 71
  Alexander C., 74, 77, 78, 81, 82, 83
Brister
  Thomas, 48
  Tom, 58
Brook
  Edward, 116
Brooks
  Edward, 114
Brown
  Jeff, 160, 162
  John E., 60
  William W., 98, 101
Brunett
  R., 46, 49
  Reme, 42, 44, 50
  Remer, 26
  Remie, 46, 49
  Remil, 31

176

178

180

Elizabeth Matilda, 121, 128
Elizuse, 90
Ephriam, 155
Evaline, 128, 150, 154
Eveline, 128, 132, 133, 137, 143, 146, 148, 157, 160
Frank, 121, 130, 133, 138, 141, 144, 147
Franklin, 128, 129, 149, 152, 155, 157, 161
Henry, 77, 79, 80, 82, 85, 86, 89
Hunaca, 134
James, 69, 71, 72, 75, 76, 78, 86, 90
James, Jr., 78, 80, 84, 85, 86
James, Sr., 80, 83, 84, 85
Joe, 128, 129
John, 129, 159, 161
John C., 148, 151, 153, 156
John Calvin, 131, 134, 136, 140, 142, 145
Joseph, 121, 125, 126, 129, 130, 131, 134, 137, 140, 141, 142, 143, 145, 147, 148, 151, 153
Louisa, 130
Louiza, 129
Lourane, 128
Lugerly, 154
Lurancy, 121
Margaret, 136, 140, 142, 145, 148, 151, 153
Margarett, 129, 131

Mary Melvina, 123
Matilda, 84, 88, 125, 126, 130, 131, 133, 138, 144, 147, 149, 152, 154, 157, 161
Michael, 121, 123, 125, 126, 144, 146, 150, 152, 154, 158, 160, 161
Milla, 153, 154
Milley, 125, 128, 131, 134, 136, 139, 142, 145, 151, 156, 161
Milly, 148, 159
Molley, 129
Oliff, 140, 143, 149, 151
Olliff, 146
Peggy, 121, 125, 126, 129, 132, 133, 138, 141
Polly, 90
Riley, 127, 128, 133, 137, 143, 146
Thomas, 81, 83, 84, 88, 92, 149, 151
Tilda, 90
Warren, 95, 98
William, 129, 156, 159, 161
William Riley, 121, 131, 134, 136, 140, 142, 145
Wriley, 125, 126, 132
Wingfield
Peggy, 165, 166
Wood
W. D., 144, 147, 149, 152, 154, 155, 156, 157
Warren D., 141, 143, 146, 147

www.ingramcontent.com/pod-product-compliance
Lightning Source LLC
Chambersburg PA
CBHW061738270326
41928CB00011B/2289